Coaching

Learning Made Simple

David Pardey

Coaching

Learning Made Simple

David Pardey

ELSEVIER

AMSTERDAM • BOSTON • HEIDELBERG • LONDON • NEW YORK • OXFORD
PARIS • SAN DIEGO • SAN FRANCISCO • SINGAPORE • SYDNEY • TOKYO

Butterworth-Heinemann is an imprint of Elsevier

Butterworth-Heinemann is an imprint of Elsevier
Linacre House, Jordan Hill, Oxford OX2 8DP, UK
30 Corporate Drive, Suite 400, Burlington, MA 01803, USA

First edition 2007

Notice
No responsibility is assumed by the publisher for any injury and/or
damage to persons or property as a matter of products liability,
negligence or otherwise, or from any use or operation of any methods,
products, instructions or ideas contained in the material herein.

British Library Cataloguing in Publication Data
A catalogue record for this book is available from the British Library.

Library of Congress Cataloguing in Publication Data
A catalogue record for this book is available
from the Library of Congress.

ISBN: 978 0 7506 8414 9

For information on all Made Simple publications
visit our website at http://books.elsevier.com

 Edited and typeset by P.K. McBride

Cartoons by John Leech

Icons designed by Sarah Ward © 1994

Printed and bound in MKT PRINT, Slovenia

Contents

Introduction

Coaching has been written with a simple purpose – to demystify the practice of coaching and put the skills and behaviours needed to coach people in the workplace within the reach of anyone who has knowledge and skills to pass on to others.

Coaching has become big business over the last couple of decades. What was once 'sitting by Nelly' to learn a skill, has become a multi-million pound industry of life coaches, business coaches and executive coaches. *Coaching* doesn't pretend to turn you overnight into a professional coach – what it will do is show how some basic (but quite demanding) skills, coupled with an understanding of motivation and learning, can help you start to coach others.

This book is loosely divided into four sections. The first two chapters look at the nature and purpose of coaching and provides the background you need to understand the role. It starts by asking 'What is coaching?' and then considers just how much of the hype surrounding coaching is justified. Chapter 2 looks at how people learn and what motivates them, essential understanding for any coach.

Chapter 3 looks at the practical preparation for a coaching programme and the initial discussions you will have with learners, and then at the structure of a coaching session. It ends by focusing on how you can plan the session to make it effective.

Chapters 4 and 5 are concerned with the practicalities of coaching. We first look at how you build effective coaching relationships, then turn to the practical skills involved in coaching. It finished by looking at some of the barriers you are likely to encounter, and how to overcome them.

Chapter 6 focuses on the effective monitoring of progress and then considers what happens when the coaching programme ends. In the final chapter, we look at the ethical responsibilities of coaching, and how you should develop yourself and your career as a coach.

Coaching wasn't written to fit a specific set of requirements, but was influenced by the demands of some of the principal qualifications available for workplace coaches. It should be invaluable for anyone working towards a Level 3 N/SVQ in Coaching in a Work Environment or the Institute of Leadership and Management's Level 3 Certificate in Coaching for Team Leaders and First Line Managers. It should also provide useful support for the Edexcel Level 3 BTEC Certificate in Life Coaching Skills and Practice.

David Pardey

2007

1 What is coaching?

What do we mean by coaching?

Coaching is a simple enough idea yet experts seem to love to argue about small points of detail as to what it is. One of the UK's leading authorities on coaching, says that coaching is:

A process that enables learning and development to occur and thus performance to improve. To be a successful a coach requires a knowledge and understanding of process as well as the variety of styles, skills and techniques that are appropriate to the context in which the coaching takes place.

Eric Parsloe, *The Manager as Coach and Mentor*, CIPD: 1999

Two other writers describe coaching very similarly, as:

A process whereby an individual, through direct discussion and guided activity, helps a colleague to learn to solve a problem, or to do a task, better than would otherwise be the case.

David Megginson and Tom Boydell, *A Managers Guide To Coaching*, CIPD: 1979

These are both fairly brief descriptions compared to the definition used by the Coaching and Mentoring Network, although some of the key points are the same.

The Coaching and Mentoring Network definition of coaching

Coaches:

◆ Facilitate the exploration of needs, motivations, desires, skills and thought processes to assist the individual in making real, lasting change.

◆ Use questioning techniques to facilitate client's own thought processes in order to identify solutions and actions rather than take a wholly directive approach.

◆ Support the client in setting appropriate goals and methods of assessing progress in relation to these goals.

◆ Observe, listen and ask questions to understand the client's situation.

◆ Creatively apply tools and techniques which may include one-to-one training, facilitating, counselling and networking.

◆ Encourage a commitment to action and the development of lasting personal growth and change.

- Maintain unconditional positive regard for the client, which means that the coach is at all times supportive and non-judgemental of the client, their views, lifestyle and aspirations.

- Ensure that clients develop personal competencies and do not develop un-healthy dependencies on the coaching or mentoring relationship.

- Evaluate the outcomes of the process, using objective measures wherever possible to ensure the relationship is successful and the client is achieving their personal goals.

- Encourage clients to continually improve competencies and to develop new developmental alliances where necessary to achieve their goals.

- Work within their area of personal competence.

- Possess qualifications and experience in the areas that skills-transfer coaching is offered.

- Manage the relationship to ensure the client receives the appropriate level of service and that programmes are neither too short, nor too long.

So what does this all tell us? Coaching is a process that mainly uses:

- Questioning

- Observing and

- Listening

to guide someone towards an agreed set of goals, usually to improve their performance or behaviour in a work role. Although coaching can be used with groups or teams, it is usually done on a one-to-one basis, and its success depends very heavily on the quality of the relationship between the coach and the person being coached.

However, it's important to recognise that there are different types of coaching, and that the type of coaching you are engaged in affects the process involved, the skills you need, the goals you will be agreeing with the person being coached and the relationships that you will be establishing. Before going on to look in detail at how you coach, it's important to establish what kind of coaching you are going to be doing. Although many of the skills you need to use will be the same, how you use them differs considerably between say, executive coaching and skills coaching.

Different types of coaches

One of the reasons for the different views about coaching is that there are now a whole range of people who work as coaches but who do different things to help different types of people address very different issues. Sometimes coaches use different titles to describe their role, such as:

Executive coaches

Almost always external to the organisation in which someone works, this type of coach works with senior managers to support them through both personal and business development. (In large organisations which are divided into semi-autonomous operations, executive coaches may work for a central HR function.) Very often the managers using coaches tend to feel isolated in their role and value having someone to discuss the decisions they face and the stresses that this puts on them.

Business coaches

These types of coaches are usually employed to help managers facing significant business developments, such as a major project or structural change in the organisation, e.g. a merger or takeover. Business coaches are often external, but can be senior figures within the organisation, and should offer a combination of business advice and personal support to the individual. They are often specialists in the task or business area concerned, because of the advisory part of their role.

Performance coaches

These focus primarily on performance, and are found in business as well as in sport and personal fitness. Performance coaching involves developing specific skills (like skills coaches, below) but also looks at wider behaviours and relationships (lifestyle issues, such as eating habits, leisure activities, work/life balance, etc.) that affect performance at work or in sporting activity. Performance coaches can be internal or external to the organisation. Increasingly, coaching subordinates to improve their performance is seen as a central part of the line managers' role.

Skills coaches

Skills coaching is much more focused on specific aspects of performance and the skills needed to ensure someone can perform a specific task. The skills coach will normally be technically very proficient in the performance of the task or very knowledgeable about it. Skills coaches can be internal or external to the organisation, and skills coaching is often a responsibility of team leaders and first-line managers, to raise the skills levels of the people they lead or manage.

Life coaches

Life coaches focus far more on personal development needs, on relationships and lifestyle, and only address work issues insofar as they have an impact on the achievement of personal goals. They are often approached by people facing difficult personal decisions or who are feeling stressed by competing pressures and are looking for help in resolving these. Life coaches can use techniques and address problems similar to those encountered in counselling, although a good life coach will be careful not to stray into areas that are really the concern of professional counsellors. Life coaches are almost exclusively external to an organisation.

Summary

What you can see from this is that coaching:

1   Ranges in focus from the *skills* needed to perform specific tasks to *personal development* and *lifestyle relationships*.

2   Sometimes relies on the coach being wholly *independent* of the person and employer, and at other times is a central part of the role of *managers* and *team leaders* in organisations.

Despite these differences, what unites the different types of coaching is that they all tend to rely on very similar skills, and it is these skills that we will mainly be looking at in this *Learning Made Simple*. However, before doing that, we'll look in more detail at the two dimensions of coaching mentioned above, the focus on skills or personal development and the degree of independence of the coach.

Skills or personal development

When we talk about skills development, we usually think of training. Because of this, coaching is often seen as a particular form of training that is done on a 'one-to-one' rather than a 'one-to-many' basis. But how does coaching differ from standard training and can it do things that other forms of training can't? An American researcher called Edgar Dale came up with a useful way of thinking about how people learn best, an idea that he called the *cone of experience*. He distinguished between learning facts or information (or 'knowing that') and being able to perform tasks at the other extreme, what he described as 'direct purposive activity'. What makes this useful is that you can see how coaching compares with other types of training at helping people to learn different things.

Edgar Dale's cone of experience

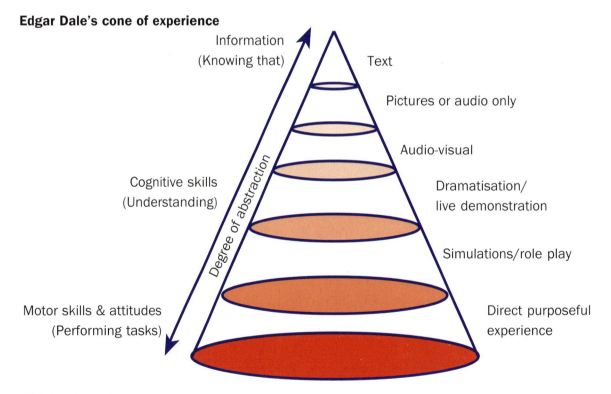

Skills development

At the top of the cone of experience is when someone learns information – as you are now. Dale says that reading texts is the best way to develop this learning because it gives you the time to stop and think, re-read passages and generally absorb the information. However, if you want to learn *how* to do something you won't do so by reading about it. Reading the rules of cricket doesn't make you any good at bowling or batting. 'Knowing that' doesn't mean that you 'know how'! Direct purposeful activity – performing a task, using skills – is the best way to learn how to do something. This is where coaching comes in because a coach can:

◆ Ask you how you think you should do something

◆ Observe you doing it

◆ Give you feedback on your performance

◆ Show you the best way to do something

◆ Discuss what you've done and how you might do it better.

That's how skills get developed. That is why skills coaching is such a useful way of helping people improve their performance at work, because it focuses clearly on what you can do and what you need to do to improve.

Personal development

By contrast, personal development is not about specific tasks or skills. It's more about the range of tasks you perform, whether this is the right range and whether you are balancing them effectively (e.g. your work/life balance). It's also about the range of knowledge and skills you possess and whether this is right for the kind of work you do and the lifestyle you want to enjoy. Although a life coach may discuss specific work situations or experiences and how you deal with them, this is largely to use them as examples of the *type* of situation and experience and how you should deal with them in future. Whereas skills coaching is focused on performance of specific tasks and being able to develop skills through supported practice, life coaching is more holistic, about how you approach certain types of situation and your attitudes and behaviour in dealing with them.

One consequence of this is that the skills coach needs to know how the tasks should be performed well in order to help the person being coached to achieve higher skills levels. By contrast, life coaches avoid leading people towards any specific behaviours; they encourage people to identify what they think is right for them and how they can develop that behaviour. The coach will help them develop that behaviour, but makes no judgement as to whether that is the right thing to do.

Colleague or independent coach?

Whether or not someone is employed in the same organisation can be very important for some coaches and the people they are coaching, whereas for others it is of very little significance. For a chief executive, an executive coach must nearly always be an external person, otherwise the coach would have to be a subordinate. Life coaches are nearly always external because people want someone to help them with their personal issues (as well, possibly, as work ones) so they are unlikely to be fellow employees.

However, performance, skills and business coaches can be either internal or external and the role could be seen as being part of a manager or team leader's job role. External coaches, when they are used, may just be a way of bringing in expertise that the organisation lacks and not because their independence is seen as being important. It's useful to make the distinction between an independent coach, who is working solely to the needs and goals of the client, and an external coach who may also be independent but could simply be filling a role that the organisation needs filling.

The greater the emphasis on personal development and lifestyle issues, the more likely the coach is to be independent of the organisation. Executive coaches are nearly always independent but will tend to focus primarily on work-related issues, so don't assume that it's a straight link.

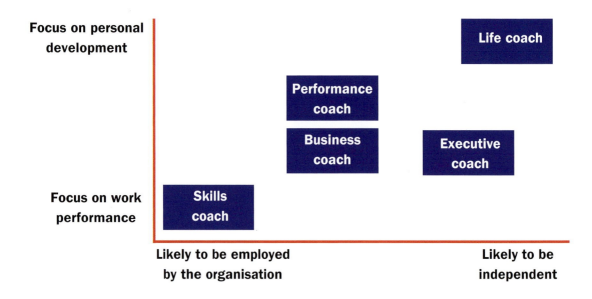

Here are some questions for you to consider:

1   Why do you want to become a coach?

2   What type of coach do you want to become?

3   Will you be focusing on developing skills and work performance, or helping people with their work/life balance and personal development issues?

4   Will you be coaching work colleagues or working as an independent coach?

You may not have any clear answers to these questions. It's quite possible that you will start your coaching career as a team leader or manager, coaching team members to improve their skills and performance, but would like to move on to become a life coach. Whatever your reason and your goals, think carefully what you want to get out of developing yourself as a coach, and what you want out of this book.

Why is coaching so popular?

What has made coaching so popular recently? For years, individual development and performance improvement (when it has been happened) has relied on training and on formal and informal feedback. Training still tends to mean going on courses, either in-house or external, although distance or flexible learning and, in recent years, e-learning have become more common. Feedback ranges from the odd comment in passing ('Well done!', 'You need to increase your work rate' or 'That's quite good') to formal appraisals.

Coaching is being used more and more by organisations and individuals to supplement these and, in the case of training, sometimes to replace them, so it must offer something, but what? Just how good is coaching at helping to develop people and improve their performance?

You can see from Edgar Dale's 'cone' diagram that coaching is going to be a much more effective way of developing employees' skills and performance than formal training in a classroom or workshop, because it's all about using people's work experience as the basis for helping them improve. And people need to improve all the time, because:

◆ People cost a lot to employ today

◆ Customers are far more demanding and able to switch to other suppliers, or complain loudly if they can't

◆ Equipment, materials and energy are expensive and can't be wasted.

However, coaching isn't a cheap solution – a trainer with 12 employees is cheaper to employ per hour, per employee, than one working on a one-to-one basis with a single employee. The coach has to be 12 times as effective as the trainer to make coaching worthwhile, and that is why coaching isn't always the best solution, or the only solution. Frequently skills coaching or performance coaching is combined with traditional training (or with e-learning) to get the best out of each method.

When it comes to executive coaching and business coaching, the benefits are likely to be greater because:

◆ Coaching provides something that training doesn't – the opportunity to focus on the critical issues facing the organisation

- Unlike using consultants, it means that the person is learning at the same time as business problems are being solved.

That's why some organisations even pay for life coaches to help employees facing challenging work and personal problems, to enable them to solve these without having to leave the organisation or finish up with a stress-related illness. The key points here are that coaching may not be the cheapest way to develop people, but it is often the most effective. Let's look at each of these points – *cost* and *effectiveness* – in turn and see what advantages they offer.

Cost

A coach usually only works with one person at a time, although some also coach teams. If a coach costs as much as to employ as a trainer, and usually they will, then the main difference in the costs of any training or coaching session will be down to the other resources used, and the number of people benefiting.

- Trainers tend to use dedicated facilities (rooms, equipment, etc.) whereas coaching normally takes place in the workplace, so training will tend to cost more to deliver, particularly if the equipment needed is expensive.

- Training means taking people away from work, often for at least half a day, which is the most expensive part.

- If there are also travel costs and, for longer courses, hotel and subsistence expenses, it gets even more expensive.

Because coaching normally takes place in the workplace, none of these other costs occur. There isn't even much loss of work, since the person being coached can be doing real work tasks, so the most that happens is that work may slow down a bit. It can also be for shorter periods, especially if the coach is a manager or team leader, who does it as part of his or her normal work. It's easy to spend 40 minutes coaching someone, without any time being lost by anyone in travelling anywhere.

However, a workplace coach normally works with just one person at a time, whereas a trainer may have six, 12 or even 20 people all learning at the same time. That's how the cost of coaching *per person* may seem to be more expensive.

1 The costs of coaching

A team leader costs £15 per hour to employ and her team members cost £9.50 per hour. She spends two hours designing a coaching programme that requires three one-hour sessions to coach each of the eight people in her team to use new software, during which they effectively only work at half their normal speed.

Cost of the coach	(2 + 3 ×8) × £15	=	£390
Cost of the learners	8 × 3 × 0.5 × £9.50	=	£114
Total			**£504**

2 The costs of in-house training

The team leader runs a half-day training session for her team. They are all away from the workplace for a little over three hours. It takes the team leader three hours to design the programme, including preparing the visual aids and arranging with the training department to have use of the room and the IT equipment.

Cost of the trainer	£90
Cost of the learners	£228
Total	**£318**

3 The costs of external training

The team are sent on a half-day course with a local IT training company. It costs £90 per person, plus four hours lost work, plus £6 travel expenses. The course itself takes three and a half hours and it takes the team half an hour to get back to work when the training finishes.

Cost of the training			£720
Cost of the learner	8 * (4 * £9.50)	=	£304
Travel expenses	8* 6	=	£48
Total			**£1072**

In this case, the lowest cost option is in-house training, although coaching isn't much more expensive. External training is the most expensive option, because this includes all the costs of the training as well as the costs of the team. But do these costs reflect the true VALUE of the programmes? That's where effectiveness comes in.

Effectiveness

Effectiveness is how well something performs, in relation to its purpose or goals. So:

◆ a blunt knife is less effective than a sharp knife at cutting food

◆ a Land Rover is less effective than a tractor at pulling a plough.

However, a blunt knife is better at spreading butter than a sharp one and a Land Rover pulls a caravan better than a tractor. So, effectiveness is measured in terms of how well something does what you want it to, it's not something that is intrinsic to it.

The purpose of both coaching and training is to change performance, although not always in the same way.

◆ **Coaching** focuses very much on behaviour – what you should do in particular circumstances.

◆ **Training** can have the same focus, but often it looks more broadly at a range of different circumstances, and teaches general principles which people then apply to the particular circumstances they may encounter.

◆ **Coaching** is generally one-to-one, so that individuals can work at their own pace and develop the skills that they need to improve.

◆ **Training** is generally with groups, working at the pace of the average, so slow learners can get lost and fast learners get bored.

In the case study, the coaching sessions are designed to ensure that the team members perform well in the workplace, bringing each person up to the standard required. If someone picks it up quickly, the coaching will finish early; if someone struggles they will get extra time – three hours per person is an average not a fixed amount. Both training sessions are fixed, and don't give each team member anything like the same level of attention. The external training will also focus on the range of possible uses of what is being learnt, not on the specific needs of the organisation.

So far we've looked at workplace skills coaching, but the general principles apply to all other types of coaching as well. You may be helping people to examine their career opportunities or the choices facing them at work or in their private life. A coach can focus on the key issues, the things that matter most to the people being coached, and help them to make personal decisions that are right for them. This one-to-one support and focus on the issues facing them are the key to your being effective.

Are there no weaknesses?

We've seen how practical coaching is, because it is one-to-one and done in the workplace, performing the tasks that have to be improved. But if it is to be effective, there must be a good personal relationship between the coach and the learner, because they work so closely together. And coaches have to be as skilled as trainers at helping people to learn.

This is something that often gets overlooked. Training, standing up in front of a group of people, even if they aren't strangers, can be quite daunting. People need to prepare for it, and may have been trained to be trainers. Coaching isn't anything like as frightening – the way many people learnt to do tasks was by 'sitting by Nelly' because all that was needed to coach someone was that you had more experience (like Nelly!). But as you'll learn in this book, coaching is just as complex a process and needs to be done well or the potentially higher cost will produce very little.

As well as this, it needs to be emphasised that coaching is all about learning to do particular tasks, not about general principles and practices, or other types of knowledge. They are better learnt through training or reading – like the *Learning Made Simple* books!

Activity

Now, here are some questions for you to consider:

◆ What kinds of performance improvements are you likely to be working on?

◆ What alternative sources of development are available?

◆ What do they cost?

◆ How could you show that you are being more cost-effective in developing people?

You may not have any clear answers to these questions but you need to think about them and look for opportunities to assess your effectiveness.

What is your role, as a coach?

You need to be clear about what your role as a coach involves and what expectations other people have of you. You need to think about the people you are coaching, their managers and those they work with, and to explore what they expect of you, and how they expect you to do it.

You also need to be clear about your own attitudes towards your role, because this will shape what you expect of yourself and others. You must consider your own motivation as this will affect how you approach the role, and also any concerns you may have about being a coach.

What do coaches do, and what do they not do?

What coaches do

◆ Agree what the learners (and interested others) want out of the process

◆ Start by focusing on what learners know and can do already

◆ Work at learners' pace to help them develop and improve their performance.

What coaches don't do

◆ Tell learners what they need to be able to do without finding out their own wants

◆ Be critical of learners' current performance

◆ Expect all learners to develop in the same way and in the same time.

What you will see from this is that coaching is all about working with people towards the goals they want to achieve, not driving them towards the goals that you have set.

1 Agreeing goals

Coaching needs to have a purpose. These goals need to be agreed between you and the people you are coaching so that they are motivated to develop and improve. People must want to achieve the goals that you are working towards if they are to learn. You can't make people learn if they don't want to, which is why they need to buy into the coaching goals.

You may need to agree goals with the learners' managers or colleagues, and part of your role is about agreeing goals that everyone can buy into. If they can't find agreed goals, there will be dissatisfaction.

You need to be clear:

◆ Who has a legitimate interest in the outcomes of the coaching.

◆ What they want from it.

◆ Any conflicts that may exist between people's expectations.

Clearly, a person's manager has an interest in a programme designed to improve performance. But managers can have expectations that are out of line with what you can achieve. Don't agree to goals that you can't deliver, especially if you haven't met the people being coached. Work colleagues may also have expectations from the programme. If they have to work closely with the person then they will be aware of his or her strengths and weaknesses. But you shouldn't talk to colleagues behind the person's back, because you want to build a culture of mutual support.

If the learner and the others have different expectations, someone will be disappointed with the outcomes of the coaching. Don't hide such conflicts of expectation because they can become more serious later.

2   Starting from where people are

You should always start from where people are – what they know and can do. Too many coaches make unrealistic assumptions about the learners and their current abilities. The greatest strength of any coach is to be able to ask questions and listen to what people tell them. The first test of this comes right at the beginning when you find out what people want from the process and where learners are, at the moment.

3   Work with people, not against them

A coach's role is to help people achieve what they are capable of, not what the coach thinks they should be able to achieve. Everyone is different. They learn in different ways and at different speeds. Some people are capable of acquiring new skills much faster than you may think – one run through and they've got it. Others seem to take ages, needing to be helped several times before achieving acceptable performance standards. Don't make judgements about someone's progress based on your experience on how other people learn. Unless you have a very good reason to suspect that someone is being deliberately awkward, you need to accept that people move forward at their own speeds.

Why do you want to be a coach?

It may be:

◆ Something you have wanted to do for some time, to pass on your knowledge and skills and see other people develop and improve.

◆ A way of building or developing your career.

◆ Part of your job that you need to be able to do.

There are some key questions you need to ask yourself if you are to understand your own attitude and motivation:

Is it your choice or somebody else's, that you should become a coach?

If you are doing it because you want to then you will probably see coaching as a positive aspect of your role, and be well motivated towards it. If you are doing it because you have been told to, you may see it as a negative aspect, resent having to do it, and lack motivation.

Have you been coached yourself, or seen other people coaching?

One effect of the experience of coaching is that you have certain assumptions about the role and what constitutes good (or bad) practice. The trouble is, you may have experienced a good coach or a bad one (how do you know?). In this book you will learn about good practice in coaching, which will help you look afresh at your own experience.

Have you already done any coaching?

You may already be a very competent coach, able to perform to a very high standard, and are looking to this book to help you improve even further. Alternatively, you may have made a very bad start, and hope it will help you overcome that. Even worse, you may not realise that you have not performing well, in which case you need to recognise that it could identify weaknesses that you weren't aware you had.

How do you feel about coaching?

Are you apprehensive about coaching, or do you feel very confident? Fear or worry may cause you to make mistakes that you wouldn't otherwise make. Over-confidence may make you unaware of your weaknesses, or lead you to expect that you can develop and improve easily and quickly.

Think about each of these questions and consider your own motivation, experience and feelings, and what they may mean for you. One of the most important parts of the coach's role is to encourage people to become *reflective*. Reflective means that they *consciously think about and analyse what they have done or are doing.* But you can't expect to encourage other people to be reflective if you aren't reflective yourself. This is a really important skill for any coach to develop and one we will return to throughout this book. You can start by using these questions to reflect on (to *consciously think about and analyse*) your motivation, experiences and attitudes to coaching. Write down your thoughts, tell them to a friend who will listen and ask questions to help you, or simply think about the questions and answers.

Activity

1   Describe your reasons for becoming a coach, your experience and attitudes towards coaching. Simply describing events can help to make them clearer.

2   What do you feel about your reasons for becoming a coach, about your experiences and your attitudes? Focus on your emotional state, and think about how that affects your behaviour and your reactions to the behaviour of others.

3   Evaluate your motivation, experience and attitudes to coaching. What are the good things and what are the bad? What do you see as your own specific strengths and weaknesses in becoming a coach?

4   Analyse the situation. What sense can you make of it? Use your existing knowledge and practice of coaching (however slim) to explain your own and others' behaviour.

5   What have you learnt about your own reasons for becoming a coach, how your experiences may affect that, and what you feel about practising as a coach? Are there any alternative courses of action? What would be the likely consequences of taking them?

This first reflective review is the start of a process we will return to. Make sure that you complete it fully and seriously, because without developing your ability to be a reflective learner (to reflect on experiences and learn from them) you will not become an effective coach.

Summary

In this first chapter we've concentrated on:

◆ What coaching is

◆ The different types of coaches

◆ How coaching can aid both skills and personal development

◆ Why some coaches can be work colleagues but others tend to be independent of the workplace

◆ The importance of people constantly improving their performance

◆ How coaching is all about performance improvement

◆ How coaching may look expensive because it's one-to-one

◆ How coaching may be a better investment if it's more effective at changing performance.

You saw how important it is for coaches to:

◆ Agree goals

◆ Start from where people are

◆ Work with people, not against them.

You were also asked to think about whether:

◆ It's your own or somebody else's choice for you to become a coach

◆ You been coached yourself, or seen other people coaching

◆ You have already done any coaching

◆ How you feel about coaching.

By developing yourself as a reflective learner you will find that you become more and more able to consider questions like these and use your answers to become a more effective and confident coach.

2 Learning and motivation

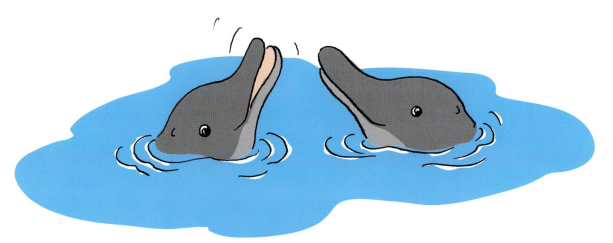

Don't you think we're selling ourselves short doing
a synchronised back flip for a scrap of mackerel?

What we mean by learning?

Coaching, when it's about helping people to develop, is all about learning. Learning is a complex and still only partially understood process, yet it's something we all do, all the time. From the moment they are born, babies start learning and continue doing it through childhood, into and throughout adulthood. There is a tendency to assume that learning is what we do in formal education, but we all learn new things every day. Some people are better at it than others, and if people are helped to learn they are more likely to do so effectively.

Learning knowledge

Knowledge is not just about memorising information; it's also about the principles that we apply to the information. Read this passage and answer the questions:

Activity

The planet Angloss has two seasons each year, wet and dry. In the wet season the Anglossians live in the upland forests eating the fruit of the bon-bon tree. In the summer they live on the plains, catching fluter fish from the rivers that are full from the rains flowing from the forested uplands.

1 Are Anglossians vegetarians, carnivores or omnivores?

2 Are the Anglossians farmers or hunter-gatherers?

If you could answer both these questions (and you probably could) it wasn't because the answers were given in the passage. You had to work from the limited information about the planet, and your knowledge of the terms 'vegetarians', 'carnivores' or 'omnivores', 'farmers' and 'hunter-gatherers'. You used your knowledge about these various descriptors and applied them to the information.

Children are believed to learn languages this way. They hear a word and repeat it (so they memorise it) and they use it to confirm that they can use it correctly – pointing at an item and saying 'chair' or 'doggie'. Parents confirm this is right or they correct their child:

Yes, that's a chair

No, it's a pussy cat

This is *feedback*. It confirms or corrects the child, and helps them learn. Soon a parent will start pointing at multiple examples and say things like:

Look at all the chairs!

There are two doggies!

This not only reinforces what the child has learnt, but introduces some principles – where there's more than one of something you add an 's'. The child then practises with this rule, making plural forms of words until she says 'Look! Childs.' She then learns the exceptions when the parent replies 'Yes, lots of children' (more feedback). You did the same when you applied your rules about categories of feeders and subsistence living to the information about the planet Angloss. This is often what we mean by 'understanding' – we can use our knowledge in new circumstances. When a child learns that the plural of 'chair' is 'chairs' she has acquired knowledge, but when she works out the rule about plurals (add 's') and uses this to make new plurals she has understanding.

Coaching is often about helping people to identify rules or learn how to use the rules to work out what to do. Although a lot of coaching concentrates on skills development it is often about encouraging people to use their knowledge and, through this, to develop their understanding.

Ben was speechless. It was obviously going to take some time to get round to 'Chocolate Easter Egg'...

Learning skills

Skills are the ability to use what we know to perform tasks. Skills are practical, not theoretical, but they are based on knowing *what* has to be done and, more importantly, knowing *why* we have to do it, so that we do it consistently or at the right time or in the right place. So skills draw on knowledge.

People learn skills in much the same way as they learn knowledge, through copying others, getting feedback and perfecting their practice. They start with simple processes or actions and then expand them or join two or more together to develop complex skills. These are of three different types:

1 Skills that involve physically doing something using parts of the body, often with tools, machines or other types of equipment, are called **psycho-motor** skills (because the brain [*psyche*] controls the physical [*motor*] movement).

2 Skills that involve mentally processing or combining information to put it into categories, solve problems or use it in other ways are called **cognitive** skills (because they involve brain activity or *cognition*).

3 Skills that involve people in relationships with others, primarily through interpersonal communication and sensing other's emotional states, and being aware of their own needs and behaviours, are called **affective** skills.

Case study

Imagine someone who has just started working in a call centre and whom you are coaching in dealing with customer enquiries. You would want him to be able to operate the keyboard efficiently and accurately, to ensure quick and accurate data entry (*psycho-motor skills*). You would want him to recognise what a customer is asking about and use the information available in the system to deal with the query (*cognitive skills*). And you want him to recognise the emotional state of the customer (*calm or angry, familiar or formal*) and respond accordingly (*affective skills*).

Coaching knowledge and skills

You can see that knowledge underpins skills – the things we do using our knowledge. Coaching can be useful at developing specific knowledge but may not be the most efficient way of doing it, especially if it is mainly knowing about things – acquiring information. Better techniques may be:

♦   Formal training

♦   Flexible or e-learning (both ways of training people individually)

♦   Reading manuals.

Coaching can be much more effective in helping people translate what they have learnt into practice, moving from knowledge to skills, and, in the process, develop their understanding. As we saw in the call centre case, a coach can often be helping someone practise his psycho-motor, cognitive and affective skills all at the same time.

How does coaching help people learn? The rule is always the same, whatever the activity – people learn best by working things out for themselves. Coaches help this to happen by getting people to try things out, asking questions about what they are doing and by giving them feedback. How they do this is what most of this book is about.

There are a couple of other aspects of learning which you should know about, to help to understand how coaching can help people to learn effectively – David Kolb's Learning Cycle and the idea of learning styles.

The Learning Cycle

An educational psychologist, David Kolb, with Ronald Fry developed a theory about how adults learn. They called this the Experiential Learning Model but it is more often known as the Experiential Learning Cycle because it envisages a continuous loop.

Why don't people learn all the time? They do! The child who works out how to make plurals hears what other people say, works out the rules and tries them out. People do this all their lives, but not as much as they could do. They fail to learn because:

♦   People don't try new things and have new concrete experiences.

- People don't notice or think about what happened – they don't *observe and reflect* consciously about their experiences .

- Because they don't observe and reflect, they don't *form abstract concepts* to explain why that happened as it did.

- Without the *new concepts* people have nothing to *test*.

Coaches can intervene at each of these stages by:

- Encouraging people to try things out.

- Asking them about them to encourage observation and reflection and lead them to work out the abstract concepts – why things were as they were.

- Try out what they've worked out to see if it is successful.

As we get into the practicalities of coaching you'll see that this model of how people learn is central to your effectiveness as a coach, so it's not some theoretical idea that has no direct relevance to practice. Quite the reverse. Kolb's idea about the experiential learning cycle is a core piece of knowledge that underpins practice. The skills that you need to use to be effective as a coach are all about helping people to work their way round the cycle.

Kolb's Learning Cycle

Concrete experience
(See, hear or do things)

Observation and reflection
(Think about what was seen, heard or done)

Formation of concepts
(Start to work out the rules – why it was like that?)

Testing new concepts
(Try out the perceived rules to see if they work)

Learning styles

Kolb and Fry's idea about the experiential learning cycle led Kolb to put forward the theory that people tend to prefer one or two stages in the cycle. This preference is often referred to as someone's learning style, which is misleading, as it implies this is *how* they learn. In fact, it is just a preference, which tends to shape *how they approach* learning.

Kolb describes four particular preferences:

◆ **Divergers** enjoy the stage from experience to reflection, generating new ideas and thinking about alternative ways of working.

◆ **Assimilators** like the reflection and conceptualisation stage, seeing how their experience links in with theories and principles.

◆ **Accommodators** like trying things out but maybe don't think enough about why things work as they do.

◆ **Convergers** are happiest doing things – once they learn about something they have to try it out.

In the learning cycle, these four preferences would sit in the corners, starting top right and moving round through the elements of the cycle.

There is a similar, but not identical, theory of learning styles developed by two British psychologists, Peter Honey and Alan Mumford, which is probably used more widely in the UK than Kolb's. They suggest that people divide into four types when it comes to learning:

◆ **Activists** like trying out new things and aren't much interested in theory, in why things work.

◆ **Reflectors** tend to listen to what people say and observe what they do and think long and hard about it before doing anything themselves.

◆ **Theorists** like reading and researching a topic before they do anything new. They would read the manual while activists press the buttons to find out what happens!

◆ **Pragmatists** are practical people who want to get on with the job and prefer to learn things that have an immediate use.

Learning modalities

The idea that people may learn better according to how they receive information (the 'mode') has been very influential but is also quite contentious. Researchers differ on its validity as a concept. However, it's useful to know about it as it does encourage you to think about how someone is receiving information and if that is the only way it can be presented.

The 'modes' refer to people's senses – we are constantly receiving information through our sight, our hearing and through touch. The learning styles theory associated with these senses suggests that some people have preferences for learning in a particular way. These three preferences are described as:

◆ **Visual** – people like to see diagrams, graphics and other visual stimuli

◆ **Auditory** – people like to hear descriptions and ideas

◆ **Kinaesthetic** – people like to do things, using their sense of touch.

These three modes – visual, auditory and kinaesthetic – are often described as VAK. (There is also a variant, VARK, that adds in Reading.)

Even if the theories are not valid, the ideas about how to organise learning that they prompt probably are valid. Coaches who are dominant in one of these areas (e.g. auditory) will tend to use this mode more when it may not be appropriate for a visually or kinaesthetically dominant learner. Instead, you should ensure that you involve all the senses, not just one, if you can. As a coach you can demonstrate an action or a task (visual), describing what you are doing (auditory) and then get the person to do it themselves (kinaesthetic).

What is motivation?

Coaching will only succeed with the willing participation of the person you are coaching. If they don't want to improve then nothing you can do will make a difference. On the other hand, highly motivated people are constantly looking for opportunities to improve and actively seek out people who can help them. You need to understand what motivates people and use this to ensure that you have the right kind of impact.

Motivation is the desire and willingness to do something. It can be:

◆   **Intrinsic** – something inside us that drives us to do something

◆   **Extrinsic** – something outside us makes us want to do something

In both cases the driver, the thing that makes us want to do something could be positive (attracting us towards a goal) or negative (driving away from something that we want to avoid).

Driver Motivation	Positive	Negative
Intrinsic	Desire to improve and achieve more, build career	Desire to avoid criticism, improve under-performance
Extrinsic	Offer of promotion by developing new skills	Threat of poor appraisal with possibility of losing job

Which of these do you think is going to make people more receptive to learning new skills and improving performance? Learning requires a willingness on the part of the learner to acquire new skills and raise performance, and that is not going to be anything like as strong if it's done reluctantly or under threat.

In his 1960 book *The Human Side Of Enterprise*, Douglas McGregor, an American social psychologist, divided managers into two kinds:

1   Theory X managers think that they can get people to perform better by shouting, threatening and keeping them under tight control. They think people only work for what they can get out of it, will do as little as possible and need constant monitoring.

2   Theory Y managers believe that people want to be successful and do their job well. Given the right opportunities they will strive hard to succeed and need encouragement and support.

In other words:

◆   Theory X managers focus on *negative extrinsic* motivation

◆   Theory Y managers emphasise *positive intrinsic* motivation

There are some other ideas about motivation but these two ideas are the most useful to coaches. You will know that the person you are coaching is going to respond best if the motivation to improve comes from inside and is driven by positive goals. If someone is under pressure from others, and fearful of failure because of the negative consequences, then they just won't respond as well to your coaching. Therefore, always look for the positives, the learner's own goals, so that they are self-motivated.

Maslow's theory of motivation

Abraham Maslow, an American psychologist, developed a theory of motivation in the 1940s and 1950s, which is still influential today. He saw it as being based on a hierarchy of needs, with the lower levels having to be satisfied before higher levels have any impact on our behaviour. You will see that some of his drivers are positive (mainly the higher levels) and some negative (mainly the lower levels). Maslow's hierarchy suggests that people driven by higher level needs, particularly self-actualisation, are likely to take advantage of the opportunities you offer for them to better themselves.

Self-actualisation
(Driver: to fulfil our potential)

Esteem
(Drivers: to achieve, be recognised)

Love
(Drivers: need for affection)

Safety
(Drivers: fear, danger, being alone)

Physiological
(Drivers: thirst, hunger, cold)

The ideas people bring to learning

For some people, learning means some of the best years of their life, at school or university. For them, the opportunity to learn is associated with positive ideas, and so they are well motivated. Unfortunately there are plenty of people who think of learning as being very negative, of being unhappy, of being labelled as a failure.

You need to know what people think of learning before you start, because that will help you understand their motivation and their assumptions about what being coached will be like. If someone thinks that it will be unpleasant they will be reluctant to learn, and unresponsive to you. What will you do? If you react to someone negatively, and start treating them like an unruly child, they will probably get angry. Since that's probably what caused the person to behave as they are, they in turn will react negatively. And the coach gets more angry. This is a negative feedback loop – a system where things get progressively worse and worse.

A negative feedback loop

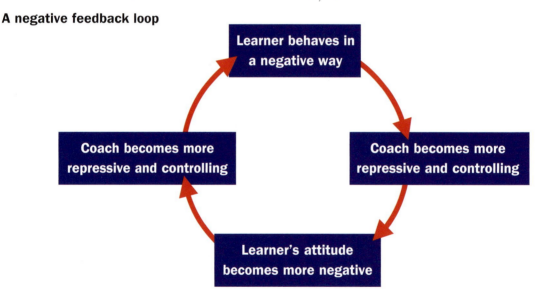

It's not too difficult to see that a positive response by a learner causes a positive feedback loop to occur – the coach responds positively and learning becomes easy. The challenge for any coach is to start off by:

◆ Discussing the previous experiences of learning – school, college and other training or coaching they've received.

- Asking what they feel about being coached – are they in a positive or negative frame of mind about being coached.
- Agree how you will work together and what you will both do and not do – this is known as a coaching contract.

We'll look at these ideas again when we move onto look at then process of coaching, but you can now see why they're important – you want to create a positive feedback loop, whereby you each respond positively to the coaching experience, and are both motivated to be successful.

Activity

1. Try out some of the questionnaires on the Internet that offer to help identify your learning styles preference. Use a search engine and look for 'learning styles inventory' and see what comes up – look for examples based on Kolb, Honey and Mumford or VAK and compare the outcomes.

2. Think about where reading this book fits into the learning cycle and what your decision to read it may say about your preferred learning style.

3. Ask yourself what your motivation is and your experience of learning. How will this affect your approach to learning?

Summary

In this chapter we've concentrated on how people learn:

- Receiving and storing information
- Mastering new information, and using it
- Getting feedback.

We have also looked at some thoeries about motivation:

- Intrinsic and extrinsic, positive and negative drivers
- Theory X and Theory Y approaches to management
- Maslow's hierarchy of needs.

3 Getting started

Goals

As you saw in the last chapter, a coach should start by agreeing what learners want to get out of the coaching process and find out what they already know and can do, so that you start from where they are.

In this chapter we'll look at these two aspects of coaching in more detail and the techniques that you can use to help you develop an outline coaching plan. A coaching plan is a tool that you can use to help you prepare for each coaching session and check out that you are helping a learner achieve the agreed goals.

One of the most widely used models of coaching, and one that we will be using in *Coaching, Learning Made Simple* is called **GROW**. GROW was developed by Graham Alexander and Sir John Whitmore and stands for:

◆ **Goal** – Coaching without goals lacks purpose, and GROW starts by making it very clear what the learner hopes to achieve from the coaching process.

◆ **Reality** – The reality is where the learner is now – their existing knowledge and skills, motivation, work role and other aspects that will determine what and how they can learn.

◆ **Options** – This is where you start discussing how you can go about developing their performance – a coach doesn't tell people what to do, but agrees with them what they can do.

◆ **Way Forward/Will/Wrap up** – There are different ways of expressing the fourth step – what should the learner do now and how well motivated are they to do it. The 'W' step involves planning how learning will take place – the 'Way forward' for your learners.

What are goals?

Goals are where we want to be at some stage in the future. Of course there's a real difference between where we would like to be and where we can actually get to, so a coach has to find the balance between what's overly ambitious or just plain dreaming, and what's so easy as to be hardly worth thinking about. Goals should be *achievable* but *stretching*:

◆ Achievable – goals that someone can't achieve will demotivate. There's no point in striving after the unachievable.

◆ Stretching – goals that are too easy don't make people try, they don't make the best use of your time and they allow the learner to coast, working below his or her full potential.

Of course, what's achievable in one session is different from what's achievable after three months, and so you need to be very conscious of the time period over which you are setting goals. This is what is meant by 'some stage in the future' – the question is, what stage? One way of thinking about this is to make a distinction between three types of goals:

Aims

Aims are the direction in which we are headed, where we want to be in the longer term. For example, someone who is currently semi-skilled may want to be come a skilled technician, or a team leader may want to move into management. A coaching programme is likely to be a step on the way to this career goal, but it won't help someone to achieve the goal unless it carries on for some time, which is possible but unlikely.

Objectives

These are clear steps on the route towards the aim and can be the goals for the coaching programme. The objectives need to be clear and precise, and should provide the learner with a clear sense of achievement when they are reached.

Targets

These are intermediate steps on the way to the objectives, the milestones along the route. They will probably be the goals for each coaching session and should show a clear progression towards the objectives.

One thing it's worth remembering – aims can change during a coaching programme, as people realise that there are other options open to them, or that their preferred goal isn't quite as attractive as it looked. This may involve you in some renegotiation of the objectives, but not large-scale change unless the learner has gone through a major change of direction.

 What is a **coaching programme**? A coaching programme is a series of coaching sessions over an agreed period of time that have been designed to achieve agreed objectives. **Coaching sessions** are individual coaching 'events'.

Setting SMART goals

You may have heard of these before. You would not set SMART aims, but both objectives and targets should be SMART.

What are SMART objectives? SMART stands for:

- **Specific** – You have to have goals that are clear, so that there can be no doubt about what the goals are.

- **Measurable** – You need to know if you've achieved them. This may simply mean that you can see that you have arrived – don't make a big deal out of this, but make sure that there can be no doubt whether or not they have been achieved.

- **Agreed** – Who needs to agree them? Certainly you and the learner, but possibly a line manager, training manager or even the learner's family, if the goals are going to involve major changes.

- **Realistic** – We've already said that there is no point in setting goals that can't be achieved, or goals that are too easy. Realistic is all about stretching someone, but not to breaking point!

- **Time-bound** – When will you arrive at your goals? Timings provide a discipline on you both – timescales can be changed, but not too often, or they become pointless.

Setting SMART goals isn't as easy at it may seem. All too often goals are woolly, which makes it difficult to measure them, or are not fully agreed so not everybody is signed up to them. Many are unrealistic, possibly because they can't be achieved in the time available, and quite often the timescales aren't clear. Let's look at some examples:

Able to use the CRM database efficiently (CRM means customer relationship management – it's what sales offices use to store customer records)	What does 'efficiently' mean? This is not measurable.
Become proficient in driving in six 2-hour lessons	This sounds quite unrealistic!
I'll tell my manager that I need six hours' coaching to be able to use the equipment properly.	This hasn't been agreed, and what does 'properly' mean, anyway?

Use SMART as a checklist and ask yourself if the goals that you have agreed are specific, measurable, agreed, realistic and time-bound, like these:

◆ Able to create a new customer file, search for customer data and produce a standard report on customers' transactions, by 3rd March.

◆ Achieve pass standard with 12 two-hour lessons or extra lessons free.

◆ Operate the equipment to the same quality standards and speed as other operatives with six hours' coaching (subject to managerial approval).

Having set the goals for the coaching programme, you now need to break these down into achievable 'bite-sized' targets for each coaching session. For example, a coaching programme for the CRM system might have targets for five separate one-hour coaching sessions as follows:

1 Open a new customer record accurately

2 Enter customer data accurately

3 Retrieve customer records in less than 10 seconds

4 Produce a standard daily report

5 Produce a standard weekly report.

One of the most important features of these SMART targets is that they build up to achieve the overall objective of the coaching programme. As a coach, one of your responsibilities is to be able to agree the SMART objectives for the programme and then reach agreement on the individual targets. You need to be able to determine how much can be achieved in each coaching session – part of your expertise is being able to determine this. We'll look at this in more detail later in the chapter.

Getting agreement

Clearly, both you and the learner need to agree the goals that you are intending to work towards, but you also need to get agreement from the other people who have an interest. For example, if you were coaching a new member of the sales team to use the CRM system, then you both need to agree what you are aiming to achieve. However, the sales office manager or team leader will also have an interest, because the new member of staff can't be very effective until the programme is complete.

The training manager may also have an interest. Your salary may be paid by the training department, and the longer you take, the more it costs them. And the company's IT systems manager may have an interest, because the more errors a new member of staff makes, the more the IT Helpdesk gets used. You may have to satisfy all these people, whose interest may differ. Some want you to be as quick as possible, whereas others want you to be as thorough as possible! You may find yourself under pressure from each to do something different. The solution to these competing goals is to be open about them and encourage them to agree what the priority should be.

One of the big advantages of coaching is that, when it's done in the workplace, you can focus on tasks that the learner can then practise between sessions. Remember David Kolb's Experiential Learning Cycle? Your coaching session provides the 'concrete experience', and should also encourage reflection leading to an understanding of what the principles are governing the task (this is the 'formation of abstract concepts'). Once the coaching session is over, a learner should apply the new learning ('test new concepts') and gradually perfect the new skills.

This is how the manager can be satisfied – the new member of the team can perform some limited tasks after the first session, and be useful as well. The practising raises performance making the money spent on you, coaching cost-effective (learning develops without you even being there) – making the training manager happy – and the IT manager is happy because the learner is only doing a single task and improving at it, not trying to do too many things.

Reality: where are you starting from?

You can't start planning a journey until you know two things:

◆ Where you are going

◆ Where you are starting from.

But do you do it in that order? Surely you ask where you are before where you are going? Funnily enough, you don't. It is quite normal to look at your goals before your starting place. Watch people using a map. They will usually look first at their goal and then at their starting point. Why? Think about the journey. Where does it begin, at the start or the destination? At the start of course, but first we look at where we want to go, then at where we are, then trace the route from the start to the end. It's the same with coaching. Agree the goals then look at where the person is now – this is the reality. From this you can tell what the journey is. If it is a long one, it may need several coaching sessions, but someone who is already quite competent may need only one.

What does 'competent' mean?

In the context of Scottish Vocational Qualifications and National Vocational Qualifications – SVQs and NVQs, competent means 'able to perform to the standard required in the workplace'. A more general definition is 'able to perform tasks effectively'.

There is a way of thinking about how people become competent, which can be useful when planning a coaching programme:

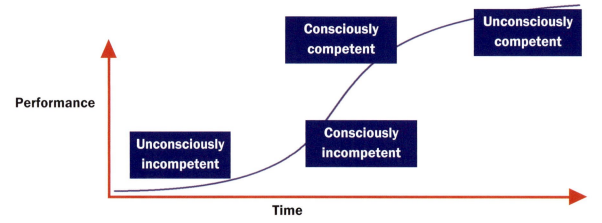

- When we start something new we may be aware that we don't know what to do but, worse than this, we don't know what it is we can't do. We are **unconsciously incompetent**.

- Once we start trying to perform a task we become aware of our lack of ability, we become **consciously incompetent**.

- As we develop a skill we become more able, but only if we think about what we are doing – we are now **consciously competent**.

- Only when we get so confident at the task are we able to stop concentrating on what we are doing (and sometimes make silly mistakes because of that). We are now **unconsciously competent**.

As a coach you will often help people make this transition, from unconscious incompetence to unconscious competence, and the starting point is to find out just what people can and can't do. This is what we mean by their 'Reality' – where they are starting from.

Training, qualifications and experience

The first step is to find out about people's formal backgrounds, the sort of things that we would put in a CV, for example.

- What relevant qualifications have they got – with the emphasis on 'relevant'? The purpose is not to go through every GCSE or swimming certificate, only what is appropriate for the task.

- What relevant training have they had, in this or similar tasks, developing skills that might be transferable?

- What practical experience have they had, again in this or related tasks, or tasks that require similar (transferable) skills?

Transferable skills

The idea of transferable skills has been around for a long time, and is used in two different ways. One way refers to those generic skills (or core skills or key skills) that are used in a range of different situations, such as communication or IT. The other is more specific, and is to do with developing a set of skills in one context that could then be transferred to a different context. For example, assembling clocks and watches develops the same skills as are needed to assemble small electronic items.

Very often people find transfer difficult. Sometimes it can be done when the skills are first being learnt, by applying them in different contexts. When this isn't the case, transfer can be helped by a coach building bridges between the old and new contexts – showing a learner how what they learnt *there* can be used *here*.

Task analysis

The second step, after you have got a picture of someone's general background is to look at their experience in more detail, focusing on the tasks that they can perform, and the tasks that they need to be able to perform. Always start with what they can do before looking at what they can't, to build up confidence and identify possible 'bridges' between there and here, opportunities for skill transfer.

In discussing what is required in the new task, you are helping them to move from unconscious to conscious incompetence, to identify clearly what it is they need to learn. However, by looking at their current competence as well (what they can do) you will help them see ways in which they can move towards competence in some aspects of the new task quite easily.

During this process it is important to distinguish between:

◆ What the person knows, and

◆ What the person can do (skills).

Knowing about something is not the same as being able to do it, as we saw earlier (in Chapter 2). Your task, as a coach, is all about helping someone to develop their performance, which means focusing on what they can do. However, what they can do is often underpinned by what they know so you need to check out their knowledge and, sometimes, help them to develop this. In later chapters we'll look at some of the resources that you can call on to do this. At this stage, it's important to be checking out what they know so that you can build on this to help improve how they do it.

Coaching styles

You can coach in different ways. You can be directive, telling people what to do, or you can involve the learner far more in their own development. There are four main styles, from the directive to the involving:

◆ **Telling** – The coach decides what needs to be done and how it should be done. The coach will assess the learners' current ability and level of performance, decide on the objectives of the coaching programme and how it is organised.

◆ **Selling** – The coach largely decides on the objectives and structure of the programme, but tries to 'sell' these decisions to learners, to build commitment to their achievement. The coach encourages the learners to ask questions about what is being done and checks that they understand what is going to happen.

◆ **Sharing** – The coach will agree the goals of the programme but encourage learners to be involved in this, asking their views and how they think these might be achieved. This is often done by offering some choices. The coach mainly defines the 'what' and the 'how' but asks the learners to help make decisions.

◆ **Allowing** – This is the most involving of the four styles. The coach describes the general goals of the programme but encourages learners to decide what specific goals they want to achieve, and how they might achieve them. The coach may well still suggest possible ways of developing skills and improving performance, but learners make all the decisions, on 'what' and 'how'.

A directive coach tries to keep control, giving few options to learners, in the *Telling* style, a little more say with the *Selling* style. An involving coach tries to get the learner to make the decisions, offering some options in the *Sharing* style and giving as much control as possible in the *Allowing* style. Which is best? If you want well-motivated learners, able and willing to learn, then the involving styles are the best to use – directive styles will create real barriers for these people. But some coaches are faced with learners who aren't at all well-motivated or interested, and they have to take the lead in setting goals and deciding on the programme. There are some learners who know very little about the tasks in which they are being coached, for whom a more directive style is needed.

You can think of these two aspects as:

◆ The **will** – how well motivated people are

◆ The **skill** – how much they can currently do.

The two involving styles (Sharing and Allowing) require the *will*, and the Allowing style also requires the *skill*. The two directive styles (Telling and Selling) are used with people who lack the *will*, but the Selling style is used with people who have the *skill*.

Assessing the will and the skill

How do you make these judgements? You have to get to know the people you are coaching. Effective coaching relies on building an effective relationship with the people you are coaching. They have to trust you and, in return, you have to understand them – their jobs, feelings about their work, motivation, their goals and their learning preferences.

How do you do this? By asking questions. Questioning is the basis of a feedback loop. A feedback loop is a process where, by asking a question, you prompt a response (the answer or 'feedback') which leads to further questions. Through this question – answer – question process you can identify someone's skill levels and their motivation (will). This use of questioning is something we will look at in greater detail in Chapter 5.

The purpose of identifying someone's 'skill' and 'will' is to help you clarify the Reality, the second stage of the GROW model, before you move onto the third stage, assess the Options open to you. The options for moving forward are the ways that you can work towards the Goals that you agreed in stage one, but the Reality is where you are starting from and this limits which options are open to you.

A well-motivated learner with a high skill level presents you with a very different starting point from one who is lacking motivation and low-skilled. Just like any journey, where you are starting from determines which routes (options) are available to you. The options aren't just the what you will cover in your coaching programme (the skills to be leant) and the order in which they can be learnt, but the way that you will coach the learner – your coaching style.

Assessing the Options

The options are the possible routes you can take to achieve the agreed Goals, from your starting point (the Reality). Choosing between the options involves you and the learner deciding on:

◆ The activities that can be undertaken to develop the desired skills

◆ The order in which they will be undertaken, which depends on the priorities for developing specific skills and the logical progression of skill development.

In making these decisions, you will also need to take into account the learner's skill level and motivation. You can expect a highly skilled learner to have both knowledge and skills that you can build on through the activities you identify. A motivated learner can be expected to work well without much support, putting what has been learnt into action. A low skilled learner might need to be taken slowly through the basics, to get started, and a learner with poor motivation will need higher levels of support and more work on your part in achieving the agreed goals.

The range of activities you can use will depend on the area in which you are doing your coaching, and you need to draw on your technical expertise to identify the range of options available. Try to build in as much variation as possible, and use manuals, handouts and other reading to develop the learners' knowledge to support skills development.

The order in which issues are addressed should take account of the importance of developing specific skills, and the urgency:

◆ **Important** means that a lot of other things depend on this being learnt

◆ **Urgent** means that it has to be learnt soon

We often confuse these two. Your priorities (which areas you address first) should reflect their urgency, starting with the less important items if you can, to get them out of the way. (The urgency of tasks should be reflected in the timescales you have set in your SMART objectives.) Then deal with important issues, the more urgent followed by the less urgent. Unimportant, least urgent issues are dealt with last of all, if at all, as these can be sacrificed, if necessary.

Do

- Think about the coaching style you are going to use

- Prepare beforehand, making sure that the resources you need are ready and suitable

- Agree your goals for the session before starting to do anything

- Work somewhere undisturbed, somewhere quiet and private, if you can, to avoid distractions and allow the learner to make mistakes without feeling foolish

- Start with the easiest elements and gradually add in complications or move onto harder tasks

- Explain things as you go along, at the appropriate point, but try to ask questions to help learners work things out for themselves

- Take advantage of opportunities to deal with important or rare issues that occur unexpectedly, where this seems appropriate and doesn't disrupt the main purpose of the session

- Give people positive feedback on their performance to confirm they are learning and to motivate them

- If learners make mistakes, use feedback to help them improve rather than to blame or criticise, and ask questions to find out why they made a mistake.

- Make the activities interesting, if possible, to motivate the learners (especially if they aren't particularly motivated to begin with)

Don't

- Be autocratic and assume you have to tell the learners everything

- Take shortcuts that the learner doesn't know about and isn't yet learning about, especially those that are commonly used but represent bad practice

- Take risks and expose yourself or the learners to any unnecessary hazards

- Take over or do things the learner could do to speed up the process, unless there are good reasons (again, for safety reasons or to correct serious errors)

- Get angry, be sarcastic, shout or otherwise let your emotions take over, no matter what you may feel inside

- Expect them to work in silence (unless they are letting themselves be distracted by others or talking about unrelated issues)

- Get sidetracked into topics you hadn't intended to deal with, unless this allows you to take advantage of important or rare opportunities

- Criticise someone for failing to achieve what you expected them to be able to do. If they got it wrong, why is it their fault? Ask questions to find out why they are having problems

- Ignore the learner, chat to others or do something else whilst you are supposed to be coaching them

Planning the Way forward

The purpose of a plan

The essence of good planning is preparing for what you want to do, to gives you confidence, particularly as a new coach. Anybody who is new to coaching is likely to feel apprehensive about doing it for the first time – if they don't, they are probably over-confident and likely to a poor job. But good planning can help you overcome any nervousness you may feel, which will make your learners confident that they can develop their skills and improve their performance.

Why do people plan? Planning is the process of working out your way forward, hte fourth stage of GROW, identifying what needs to be done to achieve a goal, what resources are needed and how long it is likely to take:

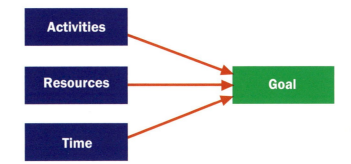

There is one thing missing from this diagram; can you think what it is? A plan is all about getting from one place or one state to another. The goal is where you want to be; the tasks, resources and time are all about the journey you are taking. What you also need to do is be clear where you are starting from.

When you start the coaching programme you will identify the learner's starting point - the *learner profile* – by doing what we have looked at earlier. You should have a good idea of the learner capabilities (the *skill*) and the motivation (the *will*). By identifying these two aspects at the beginning, you will have a clear idea where you are starting from. In successive sessions you will update the learner profile because:

◆ The learner's performance should have developed as a result of what has occurred (the skill will have changed); and

◆ You should have got a better idea of what motivates the learner and used this to improve his or her motivation (the will).

You will also have had a chance to identify what kind of coaching style you need to use (Telling, Selling, Sharing or Allowing) and, through your target setting and prioritising, have got a clear idea of what your goals are for a particular session.

The preparation work covered so far will have filled in the first (Learner profile) and the last (Goal) boxes in the diagram. What's left now is to fill in the middle boxes, which cover how you will get from where you are to where you want to be at the end of the session.

Activities

The activities are the things you will do to help you achieve the goals. These should be designed to build up skills through practice, and this is why what you learnt about how people learn is so important. You will be helping people to learn through coaching, so need to think clearly about:

◆ Moving through the learning cycle (*experience* → *reflection* → *conceptualisation* → *application*), remembering that some people favour certain stages, so need prompting to complete the cycle.

◆ Moving from what people know and can do to the new, building on existing ability and skills, to enable people to succeed.

This last point is critical – coaching activities should be designed for success, not failure. Setting people up to fail demotivates and achieves nothing, although it's surprising how many people seem to believe that there is value in giving undo-able tasks to people, to emphasise how much they have to learn. All it does it to make them think they can't succeed, and thinking you can't succeed is the way to ensure that you don't.

Belief leads to success

In May 1954 Roger Bannister ran the first 4-minute mile. Until then, it was generally believed that a sub-4 minute mile was impossible. The reigning Olympic champion John Landy had failed to break the 4 minute barrier yet, 46 days after Bannister managed the feat, Landy beat his time of 3:59.4 by 1.5 seconds. Within 18 months, 46 people had achieved times of under 4 minutes. Why could people do something that they hadn't been able to achieve? One reason was that they didn't believe they could. Once Bannister had managed it, they believed they could, and with that belief came success.

'It was simple, really. He didn't believe he could run it any faster
– so I fiddled with his watch so he thought he was going slower!'

Belief on its own isn't enough. It's not a *sufficient* condition (i.e. the only one) but it is a *necessary* condition. Part of your role as a coach is to create the self-belief that is needed for success. You can create it by:

◆ Building on existing ability, showing how skills that were learnt in one place can be used in another (what's called *learning transfer*)

◆ Using simple tasks that are easy to complete before introducing more complex ones

◆ Encouraging people to work things out for themselves (but guiding them) so that they feel some sense of real achievement.

The challenge is not to make things so simple that people feel that they are not being respected, or to guide people so much that they become dependent on you. You need to set up tasks that people can work through progressively, that offer challenges but not so much as to put people off. How do you decide what people are capable of doing? That's why the initial analysis of their skills (and their will) is so important. The time you spend finding out what people can do beforehand is time you will recoup later as people are motivated to learn and achieve their goals.

Example of task sequence

In this example, the goal is 'to enter data accurately into a spreadsheet in columns and rows; add, subtract, multiply and divide data in different cells; calculate totals using AutoSum and calculate percentages'.

Task	Reason
1 Paper exercise, using a short set of data with very simple, whole numbers	Start with something that the learner can already do – simple basic arithmetic
2 Spreadsheet exercise with the same data, explaining the idea of 'columns' and 'rows', 'cells' and 'cell labels'	Illustrating how the knowledge used previously is transferred to the new activity
3 Repeat exercise, but with a more complex set of data; introduce AutoSum function to calculate totals	Demonstrating how the spreadsheet makes complex tasks much easier, but also emphasising the importance of care in data entry
4 Discuss percentages, calculate them using the AutoSum total	Starts with what the learner knows then adds what has been learnt about spreadsheets
5 Discuss what has been covered, and how it could be used	Using the experience to encourage reflection and conceptualisation
6 Carry out activity based on new data	Practise and apply what has been learnt
7 Agree activity based on real data the learner will collect, to practise skills	Further practice and the basis for review and reflection at the next meeting

This series of activities is designed to:
- Take a learner through the learning cycle
- Move from the known to the unknown
- Transfer skills
- Move from the simple to the more complex.

Try to identify all these characteristics before reading on.

Resources

Coaching may need no particular resources other than those that are usual in the workplace. However, some activities may require very special resources. At the very least it will require somewhere for the coaching to take place, unless it is being done at a distance (by email, using an Internet or intranet forum or by telephone – all of which we'll look at later).

Privacy

Learning involves doing new things and that means that people will make mistakes. You should create an environment where people feel safe enough to make mistakes, and that means having some privacy. If it's taking place in the workplace, see if you can use an area that is away from other people. If that's not possible, place yourself in such a position that you block off what you are doing from the sight of others. Don't tolerate 'funny' or critical comments from others about what you and the learner are doing.

Health & safety

If you believe that the environment isn't safe, stop what you are doing and report it to a responsible person. If the activities involve using hazardous materials or equipment, assess the risks and discuss these with the learner beforehand. Take appropriate action to eliminate any hazards or risks if you can. Otherwise, you should minimize the risks in whatever way possible, including the proper use of protective clothes (such as hard hats, safety boots, gloves, etc.).

Preparation

You should make sure that you have prepared thoroughly any exercises you are going to use, checked them through to make sure that they work and that they achieve what you want them to. You should also make sure that you have the equipment and materials you will need, that they are appropriate for the task and that you know how to work the equipment (or your credibility as a coach will really suffer!)

Hazards and risks

Many people confuse these two concepts.

◆ A **hazard** is the potential for harm (e.g. a hole in the ground has the potential to harm someone who falls down it).

◆ A **risk** is the likelihood of the harm occurring and the level of harm that may be caused (e.g. whether anyone is likely to fall down the hole and the degree of harm that may be caused by them doing so).

If the hole is very small but in the middle of a path, the chance of someone falling down it may be high but the worst injury is probably a sprained ankle. On the other hand, a very deep hole deep in an impenetrable wood surrounded by a barbed wire fence might cause death or serious injury to anyone falling down it, but the chance of it happening is very slight. Any accident should be avoided, and you need to distinguish between those that seem so slight as not to be worth worrying about if they do occur and those that are very unlikely but if they did occur, could be very serious.

Your responsibility is to minimise the chance of something happening, however slight the harm potential might be, and make sure you know what to do it were to happen. Knowing the risk is the first step to doing this.

Time

The final part of your plan is to judge the time it will take to complete, and to check if this time is available. This is the hardest thing to work out when you have little or no experience. Things you think will take ages get done in moments; things that you think will be easy prove hard and have to be done very slowly. The best thing to do is to try out the exercises yourself (or with a friend or colleague) beforehand, but that may prove nothing – the real learner may be very different.

Nevertheless, a practice run-through will give you some idea of what's possible, and experience will gradually improve your knowledge of the actual timescales. If you prepare not just for the coming session but the session after it, you will be prepared for it taking far less time than you imagined. However, do not rush things if it takes far more time than you expected – the purpose is to achieve the agreed goals, not to complete the session in the planned time.

Putting it all together

The outline plan shown below pulls together all these elements. You can use this as the basis for creating your own plan. Careful planning ensures that you feel in control, achieve your goals and minimise any risks.

Learner Name:

Learner Profile:

- What is the learner's current skill level?
- Is the learner well motivated and enthusiastic?

Coaching style:

Session goals (SMART):

Main topics or issues to cover during the session:

1. _____
2. _____
3. _____
4. _____
5. _____
6. _____

Resources required:

- Is the location private and quiet enough?
- What equipment and materials do you need?

Health & safety

- What hazards are there?
- What are the risks of an accident or injury occurring?
- How serious could it be?
- What precautions should be taken?

Start time _____   **End time/duration:** _____

Summary

In this chapter we have looked at:

◆ The GROW model of coaching

◆ The importance of setting goals

◆ Setting SMART objectives and targets

◆ How important it is to be clear where the learner is starting from.

We have seen how planning can help you fill the space between where you are and where you want to be, identifying the activities, resources and time that you need.

You also saw how important it is, when deciding on the activities to:

◆ Move though the learning cycle, and

◆ Move from what people know and can do to the new.

4 Building relationships

The communication process

A good relationship with someone is all about effective communication, in all its different forms, so we will start looking at the coaching relationship by examining how communication works and what is needed for it to be effective.

Communication is a complex process, yet we all do it so much we take it for granted. However, doing it a lot doesn't necessarily mean we always do it well. It's like driving a car; most people would fail their driving test if they took it again a few years after they first passed, because familiarity has led them to stop concentrating on what they do. This general weakness in communication is down to four rules about communication that we ignore at our peril, according to Finnish academic Osmo Wiio. They are that:

1   If communication can fail, it will.

2   If a message can be understood in different ways, it will be understood in just that way which does the most harm.

3   There is always somebody who knows better than you what you meant by your message.

4   The more communication there is, the more difficult it is for communication to succeed.

If you think this is all a bit cynical, it probably is. Osmo had his tongue partly in his cheek when he came up with these rules, but they still ring a bell with most people. So many problems arise because people have misunderstood a message, and usually it's the people who misunderstood it who are convinced that they got it right.

Given that communication is such a critical part of our everyday lives, it's surprising that we experience so many problems. The truth is that communication is far more complex than most people recognise, and their familiarity with the process makes them sloppy in the way that they communicate with others. Given that coaching is all about communication, you need to be good at it if you are to be successful as a coach.

What is communication?

So let's start by thinking about what communication is and how we communicate with each other. Communication is the way that we transfer a message to another person (or people). This simple (but widely used) diagram illustrates this:

There are five main elements in this process:

◆ The **sender** – the person sending the message

◆ The **message** – what is being sent

◆ The **receiver** – the person or people receiving the message

◆ The **Feedback** – from the receiver, responding to the message

◆ The **channel** – this is the way that the message and feedback is transmitted and carried between the sender and receiver.

An example of communication at work

A coach (*sender*) sits down beside a learner (*receiver*) on a Monday morning and says:

'Had a good weekend?'

The learner replies:

'Not so bad. How about you?'

At face value this simple example of communication is a conversation about someone's weekend, but in fact it's far more significant. The coach is really trying to create a friendly atmosphere. The *real* message is:

You don't have to be anxious. I'm quite friendly

and the learner has responded to this by sending the message (*feedback*):

That's good. I want it to be friendly and relaxed.

After all, if the coach really wanted to know about the learner's weekend she would first have asked:

What did you do this weekend?

'Had a good weekend?' is the kind of question we ask as a way of establishing a relationship with someone, like 'How do you do?' or 'How are you?'. It's part of the process of building or maintaining a relationship.

◆ **Building relationships** is the initial process we go through when we meet people for the first time. It involves interchanges between the parties that are designed to establish what kind of relationship is to be created.

◆ **Maintaining relationships** is something we do at intervals to ensure that the relationship continues in the same way, or to change it to something new.

We'll look at both these processes further on in this chapter. However, before doing that, let's just look at the channels used in this example.

'It's for YOU!'

Channels of communication

How you communicate with people affects the way that the message is received and understood. The most common medium – or channel – of communication is through speech, but this is a very complex channel and often combined with others. In that conversation between the coach and learner, the message wasn't just in the words of the question, but in:

- The speaker's voice (both her choice of words and the way they were spoken)

- Her face (her expression and the *eye contact* she made, or didn't make, with the receiver)

- Her body (how she sat or stood – *posture* – and her proximity to the receiver).

These are all part of interpersonal communication – that directly between two or more people – and this is a combination of two things:

- **Verbal communication** is the words we use and the way we speak them (the tone of voice and the emphasis we place on different words).

- **Non-verbal communication** is the way we use our body (posture, proximity and hand gestures) and our faces (expression and eye contact) to shape the message. This is sometimes called body language, although there is more to it than just bodily signals.

It is almost impossible to separate these different channels when talking to someone face-to-face. If you want to be certain that your message isn't distorted too much, you should pay attention to them constantly.

Words

Clearly we need to use words that are clear and understood, but our choice of words, especially choosing to use technical language or jargon, or not to, can have a significant impact. A doctor might speak to a patient about his 'tummy ache' but wouldn't stand up in a lecture hall full of consultants and use words like that. Our choice of words tells people about us as much as it conveys a message, and a coach must speak to learners in language that is clear and understandable, but also precise and professional, showing that you know what you are talking about.

Tone of voice and emphasis

It's not what you say but the way that you say it. If you don't believe that, try saying the following words out loud, sounding as happy as you can and with the emphasis on the first word: 'I thought you could do that well' This is a positive, supportive statement, defending someone's perform-ance. Now say it again, sounding disappointed and putting the emphasis on the last word. It now becomes critical of the learner. Same words, different meaning. It is this ability of our voices to alter meaning that often causes people to misread letters, emails and memos – people don't hear the same voice saying them as the writer did.

Posture

Just imagine you are being coached by someone who is leaning forward, watching what you do very closely, then compare it someone leaning right back in a chair, his arms behind his head. What message would each be sending? The first could be saying:

I'm really interested in what you do or say.

I don't trust you.

The second could be saying:

I don't really care what you do or say.

I'm really confident in you and can more or less leave you to get on with it.

How would you know which is which? If the coach had just said 'I think you've really got it now' then, by leaning close, he is checking he's right and by leaning back he's showing his confidence. However, if he had said 'You're still making mistakes', then leaning forward is closely monitoring and leaning back could mean he's given up on you. Your posture as a coach can say as much about you as the words you use, sometimes more. Be alert to what your body is saying and think about the significance of the message you are sending out.

Proximity

In his classic 1959 book, *The Silent Language*, the anthropologist Edward Hall identified four bodily distances:

◆ **Intimate** (0 to 18 inches), for close friends or relatives

◆ **Personal-casual** (1.5 to 4 feet), for more general acquaintances and where closeness is necessary in more formal circumstances

◆ **Social-consultative** (4 to 10 feet), for normal work activities and formal communications

◆ **Public** (10 feet and beyond), where you are simply acknowledging each other or where communication is generally one way.

However, he also recognised that different cultures vary these distances – some allow closer and some require greater distance for each type. Also, women tend to allow closer distances with each other than with men or that men allow with each other. Most workplace activities tend to be either *personal-casual* (talking to a colleague in an informal way) or *social-consultative* (more formal discussions, especially with someone senior). Coaching can lead us to be very close to people (for observing or demonstrating), and this has two potentially problematic outcomes:

◆ We make learners feel uncomfortable by our proximity – we are in their *intimate* space.

◆ It may be seen as inappropriate sexual behaviour.

Always ask before seating yourself or standing close to a learner. You must always do so before touching someone to show them how to use their hands, arms or other part of their body.

> Be aware that people with power over us can ignore the normal social expectations about proximity – that's why bullying managers stand up close to the people they are bullying. If you are too close to a learner you may be seen to be asserting your power over them.

Hand gestures

We use our hands to:

◆ Emphasise points (by moving our hands up and down firmly or even thumping a table)

- ◆ Help to describe things (by making shapes in the air)
- ◆ Indicate things (by pointing).

The more complex an idea, the more we tend to want to use our hands to help make it clear. The trouble is, hand and arm movements (especially very large ones) can distract people from what they are doing or even what you are saying. So watch what you are 'saying' with your hands and make sure they are helping not hindering the learner.

Expression and eye contact

One of the problems with coaching someone who is engaged in a task is that they can't easily see our faces. This makes this aspect less useful, and can make communication less effective. If you want to get over a really important point, it can help to say 'Just stop what you're doing for a minute'. This will cause people, when they have stopped, to look at you. By doing this, you create an opportunity to make eye contact. If the learner avoids doing so, it may indicate fear or dislike. Don't ignore this, but follow it up (in the ways described later).

Of course, you may not always be communicating face to face. There are other channels of communication open to coaches:

- ◆ Telephone
- ◆ Email
- ◆ Online forums or chat rooms.

Each of these offers real barriers to effective communication. The telephone puts far more demands on your choice of words, emphasis and tone of voice in order to communicate clearly. Both email and online forums lack even the sound of your voice, making your words the only medium. The less time you have to think about your words (e.g. in a live chat room), the less likely you are to be precise in your choice of words. Be aware of these weaknesses and concentrate hard on what it is you want to say and, most importantly, how you want to use your words to build and maintain your relationship with learners.

What kind of relationship?

A coach has to establish an appropriate relationship with the learner – one that enables learning to take place in a professional way. A coach has power over the learner. This is down to the fact that coaches are seen to be in possession of something that the learner needs – knowledge, skills, judgement, etc. – and may also be senior in the organisation and/or in a position to affect the learner's future career.

Learners can become very dependent on coaches. This is particularly true of life coaches, who are helping people with challenging personal issues, but a coach helping someone to develop new skills can also find that the learner relies heavily on them, creating dependency or vulnerability.

◆ **Dependency** is a state of mind where one person finds it difficult to make decisions without referring to the coach. It means that someone has reduced their personal autonomy, their independence of mind, and becomes vulnerable to abuse by the coach.

◆ **Vulnerability** means that someone has lowered their natural defence mechanisms that prevent people doing things that may cause them harm or have unwanted consequences.

If all this sounds alarming, don't get too worried. This kind of dependency is rare, but it can happen, and in looking at how you create positive, professional relationships as a coach, we will focus on the actions that will prevent you from experiencing such problems.

Building relationships

Your first step in working with a new learner is to build the right kind of relationship. If you start off with this clear purpose, you are unlikely to suffer problems in the future. Here are some simple guidelines to help you.

Names

Be clear how you are going to address each other, and make sure you get the names right. Most workplaces are far less formal than they use to be – people use first names (and diminutives and nicknames as well). Coaching doesn't have to be formal, but your preferences, the learners' preferences and the organisational culture will all determine how you behave. In an increasingly diverse society, you may well meet names you don't recognise. Have the confidence to check out how a name is spelled and pronounced if you aren't familiar with it. This is easy to do at the start of a relationship, harder to do later.

Explain yourself

As you have read in previous chapters, you need to find out a quite a bit about the people you are going to be coaching. Before you start asking them about themselves, it's only fair to tell them something about yourself, unless they already know you. This doesn't mean giving a detailed personal biography, but outlining how you come to be coaching them in this way.

Explain your role

Unless people have been coached before (and even if they have), you should explain what your role as a coach involves, and how it differs from a trainer's role, for example. Chapter 1 covered that.

Be aware of non-verbal signals

Non-verbal communication can have an enormous impact on your relationship with someone. In the early stages of a relationship you can have an enormous impact because of what you do, more so than what you say. Research suggests that we make a decision about people within seconds of a first meeting, often before they have said anything. Once made, those initial impressions are very hard to change.

Be alert to the learner

The most important part of building an effective relationship is to be alert to the learner's words and behaviour. Earlier we have talked about some of the important signals people use in communication to send a message. Think about what you would expect from a learner with whom you have established a good working relationship:

◆ Smiles and laughter, or frowns?

◆ Eye contact or eye avoidance?

◆ A relaxed but alert posture or defensive, tense posture?

◆ Friendly proximity or physical avoidance?

Don't abuse your relationship

An important goal in building your relationship with a learner is to gain the learner's trust. Trust is very complex. It involves people relying on others for advice, believing that they will do what they say will do and, in trusting coaches particularly, believing that you can do something that your coach says you can do.

◆ Trust is an *emotional* rather than a *rational* state – in other words, it comes from our emotions not from a detailed analysis of someone's behaviour, although we do balance the positive and negative aspects of someone's behaviour when determining whether or not to trust them.

◆ Trust is hard to earn and easy to lose – it takes many examples of positive behaviour to build trust, but just one example of negative behaviour to destroy it. However, the power relationship that coaches have (based on the fact that they can help someone to be successful or not) means that learners feel that they have to trust them.

◆ Trust enables coaches to encourage people to do things that, under other circumstances, they wouldn't do.

   ❖ The positive result of this is that trust stretches people to do things beyond what they thought they were capable of.

   ❖ The negative result is that this can mean persuading people to do things that they shouldn't do.

As a coach you have an ethical responsibility not to abuse this power and take advantage of a learner. There are two reasons for you to accept this responsibility; if you abuse it you;

◆ May be found out and lose your job, or face legal proceedings

◆ Worse than this, you will lose any personal respect and the moral authority that you need to be able to advise people with integrity.

Maintaining relationships

Coaching relationships have a start, a middle and an end. So far we have focused on the start, but you also need to concentrate on the middle or you will reach the end sooner than you intended!

Maintaining a coaching relationship is all about:

◆ Identifying the learner's progress and giving positive feedback to show that you have recognised what is being achieved.

◆ Allowing the learner more and more control over the coaching process (moving from a more *directive* to a more *involving* style of coaching).

◆ Demonstrating through your conversations with the learner that you are listening and responding to questions and comments.

This is something you should build into your planning of the coaching programme, so that you can monitor how well you are succeeding in developing a relationship that allows learners to become less rather than more dependent on you, as coach.

The end of the coaching relationship should be a natural completion. If you have encouraged the learner to take more and more and more control then you will have less and less to do.

◆ In short coaching programmes, focused on single, simple tasks, there won't be a very substantial relationship to end.

◆ In a longer coaching programme, the more time you will have to build and maintain a good coaching relationship, so it is more important to plan how this will end in a positive way.

Summary

In this chapter we have explored the communication process and how you can use it to build an effective coaching relationship. We have focused on skills of interpersonal communication and how you need to concentrate on:

◆ Verbal communication

   ❖ Words and

   ❖ Tone of voice and emphasis

◆ Non-verbal communication

   ❖ Posture

   ❖ Proximity

   ❖ Hand gestures

   ❖ Expression and eye contact.

In building a coaching relationship you need to avoid allowing a learner to become dependent on you and abusing the power that you can have through your role. We saw how you should concentrate on:

◆ Getting names right

◆ Explaining yourself and your role

◆ Being aware of non-verbal signals

◆ Being alert to the learner.

We saw how the relationship of trust between coach and learner is emotional rather than rational at heart and that in order to develop and maintain that relationship, and ensure that it ends positively, you should:

◆ Show that you have recognised what the learner is achieving

◆ Allow the learner to take control of the coaching process

◆ Listen and respond to the learner.

5 The skills of coaching

Questioning

It's time to look in more detail at some of the specific communication skills that you need to be an effective coach. This includes the ability to ask questions and listen to the answers and how to summarise (or reflect back) and reframe what the learner has said (and also what these skills are) to ensure effective learning.

There are two main categories of question – open questions or closed questions.

◆ **Open questions** are the kind that allow respondents (the person replying to the question) to answer in any way that they wish.

◆ **Closed questions** are the kind that make respondents choose from a limited choice of answers (which may be specified or implied by the question).

Let's look at some examples of both types (about some recent training), that could be used by a coach during the initial stages of a programme to find out about the learner's background. In each case there are two examples, one is a good use of the question type, the other a poor choice. See if you can identify which is which, and why it is good or poor.

Open questions

What sort of things did you learn about on the spreadsheet training course last week?

How well have you learnt to use spreadsheets?

Closed questions

Was the spreadsheet training course just for people in the company or was it open to people from other employers?

Was the spreadsheet training course in-house for this department only or for the whole company?

I hope you felt that the first example was better than the second, in both cases. Let's look at each in turn and see what makes a good question, and which makes a poor one.

Open questions

Open questions don't make any assumptions about the answers that may be given. This means that they should encourage respondents to say what they think and feel (assuming that you have built up a good, trusting relationship with the other person). However, make them too open and people won't understand what you are asking about and you will struggle to make sense of their answer.

The two examples above illustrate this.

◆ The first question defines clearly what is being asked about (the content of a specific training course). It would be hard for the question to be misunderstood – remember Osmo Wiio's second rule ('If a message can be understood in different ways, it will be understood in just that way which does the most harm'). That means that the respondent will give an answer that will help the coach to know more about the learner's experience, which is the purpose of the question.

◆ The second question is just too open ('How well have you learnt to use spreadsheets?') If you got the answer 'Quite well', what would you be able to tell about the learner's ability to use spreadsheets? Not very much at all! Always frame questions by thinking what it is you want to know – don't use them as space-fillers, to get the learner talking but without any purpose or structure.

Good open questions are:

◆ **Purposeful** – the questioner wants to know something, and the question is designed to produce this information;

◆ **Focused** on the topic – so the respondent is clear what the questioner is asking about;

◆ **Straightforward** – not so long or complex that the respondent is not clear what the questioner is asking!

Closed questions

Remember that closed questions are those that only allow a limited set of answers. They are useful when there are only a limited number of possible answers or when you want to ensure clarity in what the respondent is saying. For example:

◆ The question 'Have you ever had any training on using spreadsheets?' assumes that only one of two answers is possible – 'Yes' or 'No'.

◆ Thinking about how useful the training course was for you, how would you rate it out of ten? (The answer to this question would be followed by the open question 'Why?')

Many closed questions are useful, because they provide clear, straightforward information that the coach can use to understand the learner's experience. However, too many are misleading because they are based on the wrong assumptions about what the learner may want to say, what range of possible options are available.

◆ In the first example, there are only two possible choices – company employees only or people from outside. Such a question may need following up with further questions to get a full picture of the course attendees ('Were they all from this department, or from others as well?' if it was just for employees, for example).

◆ The second question may look the same but in fact, it mixes two different questions. One is about being in-house or external, the other about being for the department alone or not. An answer such as 'It was open to anyone' could mean anyone from the company (i.e. it wasn't for this department only) or that it was for employees of other companies as well (i.e. it was 'open' as opposed to 'in-house').

As a general rule, it is wisest to work from open to closed questions when exploring a topic. Open questions will help you to identify the broad details; closed questions help you to confirm the details.

Other questions

All questions fall into one of the two categories we have looked at so far – open or closed– but questions can also be:

◆ Leading

◆ Rhetorical

◆ Compound.

Leading questions

These are a hybrid of open and closed questions – they are open (because respondents can choose how they answer) but closed because they are based on an assumption about what has happened and so imply that only a certain type of answer is possible.

If you have ever watched a courtroom drama you will have heard a lawyer object to leading questions, which may make you think they are always wrong. However, there are occasions when they can be useful in clarifying something that people have said, especially if they are reluctant to give a really clear answer. Leading questions are those that suggest what the answer may be. Poor ones try to put the questioner's ideas into the respondent's mouth, which is why courts don't like them. However, a coach may need to use them to get someone to say something they are reluctant to say. This could be because they don't want to be critical of someone else, or to admit to possible weaknesses.

Here are two examples of leading questions:

◆ You have been on several spreadsheet training courses, yet still seem to have problems using them. Have you not found them very effective?

◆ Was the course the usual waste of time?

In these two examples, the first question is designed to overcome this reluctance, to admit to a possible failing. It suggests that the weakness lies not with the learner but with the courses. Funnily enough, this is more likely to encourage people to admit their own weakness. Asking directly – 'Why didn't you learn from them?' – points the finger at learners and makes them defensive. Offering an opportunity to avoid responsibility often causes people to acknowledge their own weaknesses.

However, 'Was the course the usual waste of time?' is not just leading, it is judgemental. It suggests that all training is a waste of time, something that is just not true, and shows a real lack of professionalism.

Rhetorical questions

These are ones that are not really designed to be answered. For example:

◆ We all think that, don't we?

◆ Don't you wish you could always do it that well?

◆ That's not really the safest way to do it, is it?

The respondent may say 'Yes' or 'No', but the purpose of the question is more to *persuade* someone than to *obtain information* (the true purpose of a question). Rhetorical questions are effective because they encourage reflection, which is, of course, a necessary part of learning.

Compound questions

Whereas leading and rhetorical questions are useful techniques for enabling learning, compound questions tend to have the opposite effect. Compound questions combine two or more questions together, sometime nested inside each other. Examples include:

◆ Did you complete all the exercises without any problems?

◆ Have you done anything like this before and had the same problems?

What is being asked? Is it about:

◆ Completing the exercises *or* having problems?

◆ Previous experience *or* having problems?

They were both probably meant to ask about experiencing problems, but they ask two questions in one, and if the answer given is 'No' it may be an answer to the first part of either question, not the second part.

Think about your questions and make sure they are clear and straightforward, so that they produce the information you want.

Listening

We are constantly receiving information through our senses. We see things, smell them, touch and can taste them, but listening is the one sense that we have least control over. Sound is difficult to block out unless we are hard of hearing. How do we cope with the sensory overload of too much information coming in? We hear but we don't listen. Hearing and listening are two different actions:

◆ **Hearing** is passive, it happens despite any effort on our part

◆ **Listening** is active, and requires our attention.

How do you develop active listening skills? As with all things, by practice and reflection. Practice is not about doing the same thing again, but about setting out to develop a skill by conscious attention on what you want to be able to do.

If you were starting to ice skate you would hold onto the barrier around the rink and learn to balance, then try short distances on your own. When you can do that without falling over too often, you might try longer distances, across part of the rink, building up to circling the whole rink. That's practice. Walking round the rink, holding on to the barrier, only produces so much progress. It needs to be done for a purpose, to develop balance and some confidence on the ice. Once that purpose is achieved a learner has to try something more difficult.

Practice makes perfect

Here is a simple, three-step exercise to help you develop your active listening skills. You can do it with several different people.

1 Ask a colleague or friend to tell you about something – it could be a favourite holiday, film or restaurant.

2 Listen carefully and when the person has finished, ask any questions you need to check anything you don't understand.

3 Summarise what was said back to the speaker, asking for confirmation that you have covered and understood the most important points.

There are two techniques in that exercise:

- ◆ **Questioning**, to confirm understanding and points of detail

- ◆ **Reflecting** back a summary of what was said.

You can use all the different types of questioning we've looked at:

- ◆ *Open questions* to find out extra information or things you didn't really understand (How did you find out about this place?)

- ◆ *Closed questions* to confirm details that you aren't quite sure about (Did you say you were in the south of the island?)

- ◆ *Leading questions* to confirm what you think was the case but not spelled out (Were you surprised by how attractive the area was?)

- ◆ *Rhetorical questions* to show you really understood what someone means (You really enjoyed that, didn't you?)

Questioning is a valuable part of active listening and you should look for opportunities to ask questions to confirm you understand correctly, show interest and, most importantly, make sure that you are listening carefully.

Reflecting back

Reflecting back is a technique that helps reinforce understanding. It is simply a case of summarising what has been said by picking out the key points. It helps to confirm what has been said and gives the other person a chance to identify any misunderstandings. By preparing yourself to reflect back what you have heard, you will need to listen actively.

But as well as encouraging active listening, reflecting back has the added value for coaches of assisting people to learn. When you reflect back what someone has said you can:

- ◆ Correct any errors in a positive way

- ◆ Link together what the learner has just said with something that has been discussed previously

- ◆ Lead into the next area of development.

Look at the examples to see how this has been done.

Reflection in practice

Coach: 'OK Sarah, explain what you have just done.'

Sarah: 'I entered all the data into the spreadsheet, in two columns, with the labels in the first column and the numbers in the second. Then I highlighted all the data in the two columns and clicked on the graphics icon. I selected the 3D vertical bar chart and chose to make the chart in the same worksheet.'

Coach: 'That's right. Having done your research and collected the data, you entered it into the spreadsheet, highlighted it, clicked on the icon, selected the chart type, and chose where it was to be located. Well done.'

Reframing

If the person has got it wrong, or hasn't appreciated the importance of something, you need to think about *reframing* what was said. This can be thought of as 'reflection with a twist', and the twist is to change the emphasis or point of view of someone, or to correct an error. Let's look at another example of the coach and Sarah.

Sarah: 'I collected the data by writing a questionnaire and asking all the members of the team to complete it. Nearly all the questions were closed so people could say what they really thought. I then grouped them into similar types to analyse them. I should have decided beforehand what they would say as that would have saved me a lot of time grouping the different answers.'

Coach: 'So you used *open* questions because that would let team members say what they really thought, rather than what you thought they would say?'

Sarah: 'Sorry, yes, open questions. Yes, I suppose that was better, not putting words in their mouth.'

The coach corrected Sarah by emphasising the correct name for the questions she used and also turned her negative comments into a positive. This is a far less confrontational way of correcting someone. It emphasises the positives of what Sarah said and changes the negatives. This will encourage Sarah to remember both the right name for the question type and also that what she had done may have been time-consuming but it did lead to better results.

Using questioning and listening

So far we've looked at questioning and listening in isolation, but now we need to see how you can use them as the basis of your coaching technique.

The best coaching is about helping people to learn, not about telling them what to do. It works from the person and what he or she can do, encouraging learners to work out how to do things well.

I hear and I forget. I see and I remember. I do and I understand.

Confucius

When people do things for themselves, especially when they work out how to complete a task well, then they will remember that in future. Questions are designed to get people to think about what they should be doing and how they could do it.

Let's see how the coach helped Sarah to work out how to create charts in a spreadsheet in the first place.

Using questioning to support learning

Coach: 'OK Sarah, you've got your data there, haven't you. Let's see how we can use the spreadsheet to produce a chart showing how many people gave the same answers to one of the questions. Shall we use the third question?'

Sarah: 'OK.'

Coach: 'You remember how I explained that the spreadsheet is simply lots of columns and rows. We're going to create a table with the answers in one column and the data in the other. Which do you think comes first?'

Sarah: 'The answers?'

Coach: 'Yes, that's right. Do you want to put them in?'

Sarah: 'OK. Shall I start here?'

Coach: 'Yes that's fine. That's right, press Enter after each one. What happens when you do that?'

Sarah: 'The cursor moves down to the next little box.'

Coach: 'Yes, it moves down a cell. That makes it easy to add data. Well done, that's all the questions. What next?'

Sarah: 'The numbers?'

Coach: 'Yes, the data. What's happening as you add it?'

Sarah: 'The decimal point and a couple of zeroes are appearing. I'm not putting them in.'

Coach: 'No, it's because the spreadsheet is automatically doing it. Do you want them?'

Sarah: 'Not really – these can only be whole numbers. How do I get rid of them?'

Coach: 'You'll need to format the cells. Have you formatted text in word processed document?'

Sarah: 'Yes.'

Coach: 'Well, it's the same thing. All you'll be doing is to format how the numbers appear as numbers, that's all. How would you do it with text?'

Sarah: 'I'd highlight the text and select *Format* and *Style*.'

Coach: 'Right. Well here you select *Format* and *Cell*. Do you want to try doing it?'

Sarah: 'OK.'

The coach is asking Sarah questions the whole time to encourage her to work things out for herself. The coach has also used some other techniques we've looked at in this and previous chapters. Can you see them? You should be able to pick out an example of reframing (to give the right name for a *cell*), of transferring knowledge from another context (*formatting*) and of building on from what has already been learnt (in the coach's second paragraph).

A coach has to observe and think all the time. Coaching works at the pace of the learner, because if learners haven't developed a skill you can't move forward. A coach is able to develop someone's performance far more effectively than by any other technique, by:

◆   Asking questions

◆   Listening to the answers

◆   Reflecting and reframing what has been said

◆   Transferring knowledge and skills from one context to another

◆   Building on what someone can already do.

Giving feedback

Feedback is the response to a signal. A signal and the feedback can be anything – an action, a comment or just a look on someone's face. For example:

◆ When someone is doing a job well and you say 'Well done!'

◆ When someone asks you a question and you reply

◆ When someone does a job poorly and you grimace.

Feedback may or may not be intentional. A grimace when someone does something badly can happen unconsciously. Crying out 'Well done!' may not be unconscious but it may not have been intended. As a coach, you need to become more controlled in your use of feedback, trying to avoid being unintentional. This is because feedback can be of two kinds:

◆ **Positive** which is intended to reinforce the behaviour that led to the feedback being given

◆ **Negative** which is intended to discourage the behaviour.

Imagine a Victorian child rolling a hoop along the road. Every now and then the child gives the hoop a push with her hand – she is reinforcing the motion of the hoop. When she wants to slow it, she will run her hand lightly along the hoop in the opposite direction, to slow it down.

That's how feedback works. Positive feedback is like the child encouraging the hoop to keep turning, perhaps to speed it up. Negative feedback is like the reverse motion, slowing the hoop down. However, when dealing with people, there is a complication. Unlike hoops, people have feelings. Positive feedback produces a positive emotion making people feel better about themselves, perhaps feeling some pride in their achievement. If you look back to Maslow's ideas about motivation (page 29), you will note that he saw esteem as one of the higher level motivators.

◆ Positive feedback is all about demonstrating *esteem* (or respect) for someone, encouraging that person to develop their own self-esteem, their feelings about being valued and valuing themselves.

◆ Negative feedback has the opposite effect, reducing someone's self-esteem and sense of being valued by others.

This is evident in the way that people react to feedback. Positive feedback encourages people to be happy, to relax, to feel some pride in themselves (and possibly to blush). Negative feedback can produce very different reactions. People tense up, become unhappy or even angry, and although they may get red in the face they aren't blushing with pride, but with anger! The anger may be directed at themselves, but it can just as easily be directed at the person who has criticised them.

Emotional responses are important, but it's also important to recognise how feedback enables people to learn and develop. Most people don't like to take too many risks, so they don't try out new things very often. If you want to get someone to try something they haven't done before, it is easiest to get them to move gradually from the old to the new. However, the old ways are often very firmly entrenched – it's as if the Victorian child's hoop is stuck in a tramline. It can go forward, stop or go back, but it can't easily change direction.

> If you always do what you've always done, you'll get what you've always got!

Often, no feedback is taken as positive feedback, and people keep doing what they have always done because nobody has told them not to. Often your job is to help people change from doing what they have always done, but by giving them positive feedback on their efforts to get out of the tramline they are fixed in, not negative feedback on being stuck there.

Rules for giving effective positive feedback

- ◆ Focus on the person and what they have achieved, not what others can do.
- ◆ Identify improvements, however small, and make positive comments.
- ◆ When things haven't worked properly, emphasise how much harder it often is to relearn than it is to learn for the first time.

You should also be ready to talk about the person's feelings as well as their actions – they have a right to feel anxious so acknowledge that, and emphasise that they are doing well to overcome this. Emotions matter, far more than we often recognise.

Understanding emotions

People feel lots of different emotions, all the time. Emotions are an immediate response to external stimulus – something we see, here or do. They aren't controlled by the rational part of the brain but are the result of an instinctive reaction in one of the most primitive parts of the brain, called the *amygdala*. This is useful in primitive societies, where danger lurked around the corner – the 'fight or flight' response is triggered by the amygdala seeing a danger and stimulating an immediate reaction.

Emotions often exist along a range of dimensions, such as:

These aren't the extremes, either. Beyond 'happy' there is 'ecstatic'; beyond sad there is 'deeply depressed' and between these extremes there are various degrees of happiness and sadness. We feel these emotional responses all the time, and can switch quite quickly from one to another. Some people tend to react far more emotionally to events than do others, whereas some people appear very unemotional and unresponsive. You need to be alert to these different kinds of emotional responses in people, and in yourself.

If someone is very emotional they may react far more strongly than you would expect to your feedback. Alternatively, some people may not seem to be at all aware of your feedback, because they show no emotional reaction. Don't confuse their lack of an emotional response to a lack of understanding of your feedback. The ability to recognise your own and other's emotional states is what is meant by *emotional intelligence.*

What is emotional intelligence?

John Mayer and Peter Salovey first came up with the idea of emotional intelligence in the 1980s and 1990s (most significantly in their paper 'Emotional intelligence' in *Imagination, Cognition and Personality*, volume 9).

They identified four main dimensions of emotional intelligence:

◆ **Emotional perception and expression** – the ability to identify emotion in oneself and in other people, to express emotions accurately and to discriminate between real and artificial feelings.

◆ **Emotional facilitation of thought** – the ability to use own and others' emotional states to positively help rather than hinder rational thinking.

◆ **Emotional understanding** – the ability to understand how emotions affect and relate to each other, and how changes in emotions occur.

◆ **Emotional management** – the ability to be open to our feelings, and to manage them and the emotional responses of others.

In other words, emotional intelligence is simply the ability to recognise how you and other people feel, to use your feelings constructively, and to take action to ensure that you and others are experiencing positive emotions to achieve your goals. How, as a coach, can you do this to enable people to learn and develop successfully?

Working with emotions

We experience different levels of emotion at different times and in response to different stimuli. What can make you feel mildly disappointed one day can cause you to feel very depressed on another. This is because your state of mind and your physical state (for example, if you're tired) will affect how you react to the stimuli that are causing your emotional reactions.

Emotional intelligence means being aware of this (what Mayer and Salovey call *emotional understanding*). It also means recognising how our emotions affect us, both behaviourally and physically.

◆ **Behavioural**, in that the emotion causes us to behave in a particular way.

◆ **Physical**, in that our body generates a neuro-chemical response – it sends signals through our nervous system and to our hormonal system.

If you give someone positive feedback, they may well look pleased, by smiling and looking you in the eye (a behavioural response). They may also blush (a physical response over which they have no control). As a coach you need to recognise this emotional response in others, and also be aware of your own emotional reactions (Mayer and Salovey's *emotional perception and expression*). If someone is slow to develop a skill you might find yourself getting angry and need to be able to recognise this and to control or channel the emotion to avoid it affecting your relationship with the learners (Mayer and Salovey's *emotional management*).

In a modern, complex society, we are often presented with a wide range of situations that cause us to have rapidly changing emotional states.

◆ A bad car journey causes frustration or anger

◆ Abusive customers can cause unhappiness or fear

◆ Colleagues who seem to be more successful can cause jealousy.

An effective emotionally intelligent coach, needs to learn how to control these emotional responses, but this is difficult. One result of this difficulty in coping with different emotional states is that we get conflicts between our emotional responses and what we know we should do, something that can cause people to experience *stress*. Understanding emotions is the first step to being able to control them more effectively without experiencing stressful pressures.

Anchoring your emotions

This exercise is a useful one to help you recognise how emotional states occur.

1   Think back to an experience you have had that was very joyful. It could be getting married, winning a race, having a first child.

2   Think hard about the actual experience (it can help if you shut your eyes) and try to imagine yourself in the particular place and at the time when you first had the experience.

3   If you really focus hard on the circumstances you may well find that the same emotional state will be recreated. You should feel a strong sense of well-being and self-esteem; you may even feel tears in your eyes.

This is a technique known as *anchoring* – stimulating an emotional response through thinking hard about the particular situation where that emotion occurred. It means that the rational mind (where you think about the situation) is stimulating the amygdala to respond.

If you start by using very significant emotional states, you will find that, with practice, you can more readily stimulate the emotional reaction. Then, by using less emotionally charged situations, you should learn to anchor different emotions in a range of different situations. This will help you gain some control over your emotions and become less controlled by them.

This is not about desensitising yourself – you are still feeling emotions, just having some control over which emotions. In the process, you can learn to reduce the stress that comes from conflicting or unpleasant emotions, and use your emotional state to help you in your relationships with others. What it isn't about is trying to pretend to emotions you don't feel – that would be dishonest, and prevent you from building up trust.

Coaching is based on trust

Trust is fundamental to a successful coaching relationship.

◆ The people you are coaching must trust you if they are to learn effectively and to rely on your guidance and advice.

◆ You must trust those you coach to carry out tasks they have agreed to do and develop their performance.

Trust is about the confidence that people have in each other, leading them to be open about their fears and feelings and to rely on others for support. Trust is often very hard to build, especially from someone who has been let down in the past, and yet it's very easy to lose. Why are some people ready to trust others, and what makes somebody trustworthy?

Trust depends on:

◆ **Consistency** in your attitudes and behaviour.

◆ **Honesty** - if you lie and get found out (and you will sometimes) then who is going to believe you again?

◆ **Openness** - people who appear to have something to hide don't inspire trust.

Too often coaches attempt to build a relationship by pretending to attitudes that they think others will prefer them to have. Or else they try to appear more knowledgeable or confident than they are, because they don't want to admit to a weakness. Unfortunately, they will either show themselves up as dishonest or that they lack openness.

Coaches who want to build trust need to be able to:

◆ Share information, especially about themselves

◆ Listen to others, acknowledging any ignorance or mistakes

◆ Be fair, not show favouritism or unevenness in their behaviour

◆ Keep their promises

◆ Recognise other people's abilities and show interest in them

◆ Trust others - they won't trust you if you don't trust them.

If you can do this, you will be able to build a relationship based on trust. Your ability to get people to do things they didn't know that they could do will be strengthened and your feedback will be welcomed.

Building rapport

Rapport is an elusive concept. It is easier to recognise than to describe, but we'll have a go. It can be thought of as the state a relationship reaches when two people have achieved a harmony in their thinking and really understand each other well, with minimal effort on either part. You can see rapport when two people have been together a long time and are able to communicate together effortlessly and with the minimum of words. They will instinctively look at each other and communicate with facial expressions when some one says something that they know they will both feel the same way about.

You don't have to work with someone for years to establish this kind of rapport, but you can achieve a rapport with someone in far less time, if you try hard. And it's worth trying hard, because a sense of rapport between you and the learner means that you will be able to communicate more easily and effectively.

Ways to build rapport:

◆ Asking questions (and doing so in a way that demonstrates a clear interest in other people and what they can do)

◆ Listening actively (to understand their answers to your questions)

◆ Reflecting back and reframing their answers (to show you are listening and to emphasise the positives)

◆ Giving feedback (in a clear and honest way, that will help them learn and develop

◆ Listening to their feedback to you (to show that you value their views)

◆ Recognising their emotional states and your own (and using this knowledge to improve communication)

◆ Behaving in ways that will earn their trust (and also show you trust them).

If you can focus on doing this you will develop an effective coaching relationship and help those you are coaching to learn and develop successfully.

Overcoming barriers

Coaching is all about the relationship between the coach and the learner, something that has been explored in some detail in earlier chapters, and any barriers to that relationship can have a serious impact on the effectiveness of your coaching activity.

However, that doesn't mean that there are no external factors, or that they can be ignored. Coaching doesn't happen in a vacuum, but usually takes place in a working environment where all sorts of barriers can arise. We'll start by looking at the organisational barriers, because they can also cause some of the personal barriers, before moving on to look at those.

Organisational barriers to coaching success

There are seven specific barriers that you are likely to meet, each of which is examined below, but they all arise from one broad cause - a lack of commitment to the idea of coaching as a way of significantly improving performance. Although it's possible to address some of the specific barriers that you encounter, this is the one that really needs addressing,.

The specific barriers that you are likely to encounter are:

◆ **Lack of time** - This is frequently a problem in more authoritarian organisations, where managers want things done quickly and in their way. Coaching can seem to be slow (as not everyone can participate at the same time, as in formal training) and it may be something they are unfamiliar with and feel uneasy about. The emphasis in coaching on asking questions and working from the learners' needs runs contrary to the 'command and control' attitude of an authoritarian management style.

◆ **Fear of the skills used in coaching** - This is related to the first barrier. Managers who can't coach - or don't know what coaching is - will tend to oppose its use. The insecurity that many feel when considering the use of coaching reveals a deeper uncertainty in their managerial role. Weak managers think they should know everything while knowing that they don't. They often hide this weakness by not valuing the things they can't do themselves.

◆ **Fear of employees** – This is an even more advanced case of the previous one, where managers are scared of the people they manage, perhaps because of their insecurity in their role and/or the skills and abilities of others. They may fear telling people that there will be a coaching programme in case people argue against the need, or are fearful that higher skills will give people even greater advantage over them.

◆ **Fear of the coach** – If the coach can do something that a manager can't do, then the coach can present a threat to the manager. Bundle this up with a fear of employees and of risk, and there can be an enormous resistance to the coaching programme.

◆ **Fear of risk** – Coaching costs money, as we have seen, and managers may not be sure that it will produce the benefits needed. This is even more pronounced if there has been a previous use of coaching and it didn't bring the results expected.

◆ **Unwillingness to recognise difficult performance issues** – This is linked to the general fear of employees, but more specific. Having an under-performing employee can be a major challenge for managers who are reluctant to address these problems. For some, a coach is a useful way of avoiding the challenge, passing it on to someone else, but others would rather avoid the problem altogether, in the hope that it will go away. First of all, it means telling someone they are under-performing (the first hurdle for the manager to overcome) and then, if the coaching fails to change someone's behaviour, having to take more drastic action.

Individual barriers to success

David Clutterbuck, one of the leading authorities on coaching, said that 'Coaching works best when the *coachee* is both a willing and an informed participant.' He goes on to argue that people will learn far more if they understand what is happening and how they can benefit by being able to ask questions in a way that will ensure that they get the help they need.

This assumes that people accept the idea that they have to learn, and this is hardest where someone is under-performing and coaching is being used to address these problems. Coaching is seen as a threat, not the best basis for an effective coaching relationship!

Other barriers include:

- **Poor personal relationship** – Not all learners and coaches get on. Different personalities, attitudes or beliefs can make it hard for you to establish an effective coaching relationship.

- **Fear of failure** – If you are trying to help someone to do a task in a new way, they may resist learning in case they get it wrong. It is often harder to learn to do something differently than to do something completely new.

- **Fear of extra work** – You will often coach people in new tasks that are in addition to old ones. The reluctance to learn is a defence mechanism to avoid becoming overloaded with work – after all, if they can't do it they can't be expected to do it.

- **Fear of appearing incompetent** – People can't hide any problems in a one-to-one situation (unlike in group training). The more experienced people are, the greater this fear can be – someone new to a role doesn't expect to be able to do it straightaway.

- **Fear of change** – This is often a result of the fear of failure, but made worse by the sense that there are no certainties left in the workplace, if the coaching programme is to learn new skills as part of a wider set of changes. The fear is not just related to what you are doing, but just a part of a wider set of fears.

- **The perception that coaching is therapy or counselling** – Where coaching is part of a broader strategy, not purely for skills development, then people may be fearful that they will be expected to discuss personal issues that impact on their work performance. Of course, that may be something they should do, but we've already seen how important it is for coaches to avoid addressing issues beyond their competence, because you are not a therapist. The people you are coaching may not be aware of the boundaries that you will be setting on the coaching relationship.

Overcoming barriers to success

If this list of barriers look overwhelming, don't let it overwhelm you because most of them arise from similar sources and can be addressed with a few basic strategies, most of which we have introduced already. If you approach the coaching programme in the way advocated in this book, you'll find that this will help to overcome many of the barriers.

1   The starting point is to recognise that many of these barriers are about perceptions not realities. The fear that managers and learners have of the unknown are best overcome by clearly explaining what coaching involves and how it works.

2   Present the time spent in coaching as time when work is still being done, not as lost time. Emphasise that coaching is about real work, in the workplace, and leads directly to change and improvement.

3   Work on creating an effective relationship right from the start, using the techniques that you will be using when coaching – ask questions, listen carefully, make the learner the centre of the process so that they feel valued and confident.

4   Use the same techniques with managers, so that you can find out about their goals and their fears, and lead them towards a positive frame of mind by getting them to work out how they will benefit by having more effective people working for them.

5   Start from what people can currently do and build on that. Give people confidence in their own skills and performance before introducing anything new. Use positive feedback early and often, to reinforce success and give greater confidence in their ability to learn and improve.

In other words, if coaching is done properly and well, then most of the barriers will disappear. Many coaches, especially when they are new to the role, find that they slip back into a 'telling' style when barriers first appear, as a defence mechanism. This is because most people have previously learnt in that way, and it is one people feel at home with. Unfortunately, it isn't necessarily the best style to use and is least effective at bringing about significant and lasting change.

In the early stages of being a coach you will benefit from having a coaching supervisor who can help you concentrate on implementing the best practice in coaching. It is also helpful to have someone more experienced available to help you if the barriers seem too great to overcome.

Summary

In this chapter we have pulled together the skills you need to be effective as a coach. We have seen:

◆ How to use different types of questions to achieve different things.

◆ That questioning is no good without active listening.

◆ The importance of developing a successful relationship with the people you are coaching.

◆ The importance of emotions and the need to develope your emotional intelligence.

◆ That a coach must be trusted, which depends on your consistency, honesty and openness.

We have looked closely at some of the barriers to coaching that you are most likely to meet, both organisational and individual barriers, and seen that the best way to overcome these barriers is through best practice in coaching.

6 Reaching the end

Recording learning

How well are learners doing in achieving their goals? How well have they developed their skills and improved their performance? Are they able to work to the standards required for effective performance? These are all questions that a coach needs to be able to answer, and that means that you need to be able to monitor a learner's progress.

Although it may seem obvious, it is important to keep records of what has been covered in a coaching session. You may well feel that the plans that you made for it are sufficient for this purpose, but it's useful to recognise that what you plan and what you do aren't always the same thing.

The best laid schemes o' mice an' men, gang aft a-gley.
Robert Burns

Why do things *'gang agley'*? Why do our plans not work out in practice?

◆ Sometimes they were the wrong plans – you can't always get it right, but if they often turn out to be wrong then it probably is something to do with your planning. You may have tried to do too much, it may have been the order, or you may have under-estimate the learner's ability.

◆ Events occur that we hadn't planned for. Coaches should be responsive to the needs of learners and these can be hard to forecast. Something may have happened since the last session and they have waited for you to help them to solve their problem.

Sorry, Rab –what does 'gang aft a-gley' mean?

- Opportunities arise unexpectedly that offer a chance to do something unplanned, and that it would be foolish to ignore. It could be something very rare, or an opportunity so appropriate, that the learning would be far better than anything you could plan.

Not following a plan exactly is a strength, not a weakness. When you are new to coaching you may feel uncomfortable if you don't keep closely to your plans, but with experience you will learn to be more flexible. But it does mean that the plan may not be an accurate record of what happened.

 It's one thing to ask learners about the previous session to help them recall what was done, it's another to do it because you've forgotten. This looks unprofessional. It's also rude and shows that you don't take interest in what you have been doing.

What should you record?

After each coaching session you should record when and where the coaching took place and, as well as this, you should also record:

- The **activities covered** – with a note about anything that was unplanned, why it was covered and whether it still needs to be addressed in more detail at a planned time.

- The **outcomes**, with an assessment of how well the learner had achieved the required standard, and aspects still to be completed.

- Any **practice** that the learner is to undertake before the next session, to develop skills or understanding, or to find information.

- Any **tasks** you have undertaken to do before the next session. This may include finding out information, collecting resources, seeking agreement for the learner to undertake certain tasks.

- Any topics to be addressed in the **next** session. This could be to complete something or a new area that the learner has identified.

These five aspects are all you need to record and should provide an effective checklist when preparing for the next session. You need to keep these records appropriately. Never record anything that you would not want the learner to read. This means that you should only record what you have done or seen, not what you have thought or assumed about the learner.

Review outcomes

It is useful to spend time at the end of a session to review with the learner:

◆ What you had planned to do

◆ What you actually did.

Note this down, agreeing with the learner what you covered (*activities*) and how they performed (*outcomes*), what each of you will be doing before the next session (*practice* and *tasks*), and when that is and what will be covered (*next*). If you start a session by discussing what is going to be covered, and finish it by looking at what you actually did, it helps learners to set their learning into context.

Coaching is a partnership between the coach and learner. You both need to be engaged in the process. If you keep private records it implies that you are doing the coaching **to** the learner, not working **with** the learner.

The review both ends the session and provides the basis for the next. You can use the record to start the next session by reviewing the activities and outcomes, finding out if the learner has been able to practise as agreed, and if you have done what you agreed to do. Then you can agree what you are going to do in this session – and start doing it.

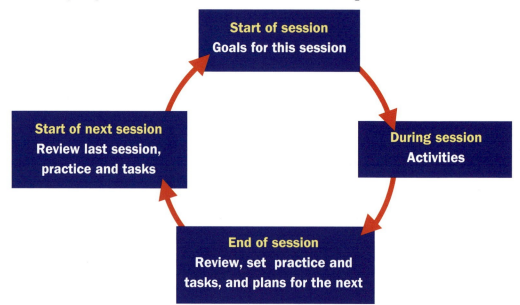

This cycle - **Plan-Do-Review** - is a firm basis for any learning. However, it can only work if you have a plan and if you are able to look back at what you have done (review) - which is why you need to record it.

Assessing learning

Assessment is the process by which a person's performance is compared to a standard or set of criteria which they are expected to achieve.

◆ Who decides what these standards or criteria are?

◆ How do you judge performance against them?

Assessment can be formal, leading to someone gaining a qualification or being certified competent to carry out critical tasks, or it can be informal, to confirm that the coaching programme has been completed satisfactorily. The same principles and practices apply to both.

Performance standards and criteria

Some organisations have developed their own performance standards or criteria – you may have been involved in doing this as part of the preparation for the coaching programme. But, there are national standards for many of the jobs that people do. These **National Occupational Standards** (NOS) are the basis for many qualifications and they can also be used for many other purposes, including job descriptions and as the basis for judging employee performance.

You can find out about the NOS for your area of activity from the website **http://www.ukstandards.org**. You will find references there to two different types of organisations that are responsible for NOS:

◆ Sector Skills Councils (SSCs) – are Government-sponsored organisations bringing together representatives of the major employment sectors, which have responsibility for setting the standards and agreeing skills development strategies for their sectors.

◆ Standard setting bodies – operate in specialised areas of different sectors, setting standards for SSCs, or in the few areas for which there is no SSC (mainly for occupations that are found across employment sectors, such as management or administration).

If you are an assessor for a formal qualification then specific rules will have been set by the awarding body that affect what you do and how you do it. You would be trained in these techniques as part of your preparation for the role.

UK qualifications

There are two main types of qualifications found across the UK.

◆ National Vocational Qualifications (NVQ) or, in Scotland, Scottish Vocational Qualifications (SVQ) are based on the assessment of occupational competence.

◆ Vocationally Related Qualifications (VRQ) don't require learners to demonstrate that they *can* perform the role in the workplace, but that they know *how to* and have the necessary skills.

To find out about qualifications across the UK, the best places to look are:

◆ www.sqa.org.uk (for Scotland)

◆ www.accreditedqualifications.org.uk (for the rest of the UK)

The basis for all assessment, is the same – how well does performance match the standard. This should be based on the highest quality of work while allowing for the nature of the job role. You can't expect the same standard for servicing equipment from a semi-skilled machine operator as you would from a highly skilled fitter. Different people may perform the same task to different standards, and must be assessed accordingly.

◆ As part of your initial planning for a coaching programme you should discuss these issues and be clear what standard is expected and ensure that this is reasonable for the people involved.

◆ You should also make sure that the learners know what is expected of them and how their performance will be judged.

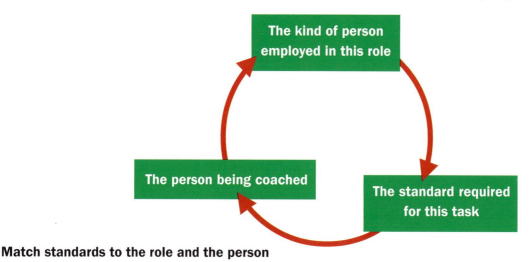

Match standards to the role and the person

Making assessment decisions

In making assessment decisions you are making a judgement, and that places a significant pressure on you to be:

◆ **Honest** – the judgement you make should be your own, not swayed by your desire for the learner to 'pass' or 'fail' the assessment. All performance assessment is subjective, no matter how objective the standards in use, and it is your opinion about the learner's performance compared to these that is required, based on your experience and your integrity.

◆ **Fair** – you shouldn't allow your feelings about the person or the organisation to sway your judgements. Don't allow age, sex, race, ethnicity, religion, sexuality or disability to affect your judgement. There is one slight exception to this, where a disability means that performance depends on the use of special equipment. If the person can perform effectively with this additional assistance then they are being judged against the same standards as others, and the assessment is still fair.

◆ **Accurate** – you should make sure that you are familiar enough with the standard and attentive to the learners' performance that you can make a judgement based on both. A cursory glance at the standards two months ago is not enough to make an accurate assessment today. You should normally have the standards in front of you when making a judgement about someone's performance.

This assessment could be taking place at stages during a coaching programme to identify how well someone is progressing towards their final goal. This is usually described as *formative* assessment. The assessment could also be at the end of a programme, or at a significant stage in it, when a particular area of development activity has been completed. This is known as *summative* assessment.

◆ **Formative assessment** should be designed to help learners know how far they have progressed and what they still need to do. It is part of the development process, a way of giving feedback.

◆ **Summative assessment** should be designed to demonstrate completion of a stage of learning and not undertaken until you are confident that the learner can meet the standard. Although it is also feedback, it is more about confirmation and completion.

In both cases your judgements should identify:

◆ What the learner can actually do – which aspects of the performance standards or criteria is being met.

◆ What the learner still needs to learn or improve on.

Ideally, summative assessment should only identify what someone can do; formative assessment is used to identify what else still needs to be done. If you were assessing for an SVQ or NVQ you would say, in the latter case, that someone is 'not yet competent'.

As a coach you are helping people to develop and you should use assessment to help this process. There are some people who feel that assessment should always produce failures as well as successes, because that's their definition of high standards. This is intellectually flawed:

◆ High standards and high quality coaching or training can produce 100% success.

◆ Low standards and poor quality coaching or training can produce 100% failure.

If standards are set at the right level, and if people are being well coached to improve their performance, then success is always possible. Failure to achieve standards occurs if:

◆ The wrong standards are being used

◆ The coaching is not good enough

◆ The learners lack the motivation or ability to achieve.

You can ensure that the right standards are used in your initial planning. You can develop your performance as a coach. You can make sure that people are capable of achieving through your initial diagnostic processes and through your support and guidance to help motivate them.

The end is nigh!

Your coaching programme started with a set of goals. It ends when those goals have been achieved, or when no more progress is possible. This is the point where you should review your programme, with the learner, to see what you have achieved and how much progress you have made.

The place to start your review is the place you started your coaching programme, the goals that you agreed. You should sit down with the learner and examine:

◆ What the original goals were

◆ Any changes were made during the course of the programme

◆ What you had achieved by the end of the programme.

In Chapter 3 we said that goals should be achievable but stretching. You should expect that your agreed goals have been more or less all achieved. If they haven't then you need to ask whether or not they were realistic in the first place. If they have been very well achieved, perhaps in less time than expected, or have been exceeded, you need to ask if they were stretching enough.

We also said, in Chapter 3, that goals can be of three kinds:

◆ **Aims** – where we want to be in the longer term.

◆ **Objectives** – clear steps on the route towards the aim.

◆ **Targets** – steps on the way, the goals for each session.

At the end of the coaching programme it is the *Objectives* that you will be reviewing. However, in the process, you could also look at the *targets* for each coaching session. This will help you to find out why any objectives were missed, if they were.

We introduced the idea of the progression from *unconscious incompetence*, through *conscious incompetence* and *conscious competence* to *unconscious competence*. People have to realise what they can't do before learning how to do it, then internalise what they have learnt so they can do it naturally. By the end of the programme you should have reached the *conscious competence* stage and the learner needs to practise the new skills enough to be able to use them without thinking too much about it.

What do you do now?

We've already seen that the goals that were discussed at the beginning of the programme will have included longer-term aims. Now is the time to look again at those aims and discuss what the learner would like to move onto. That doesn't mean starting a new coaching programme (although that may be possible) but looking at the range of possibilities open to them. This could include:

◆ Attending a course or series of short courses

◆ Using flexible (paper-based) or e-learning (computer-based)

◆ Reading and researching

◆ Seeking a work placement or job shadowing

◆ Seeking promotion or a job change

◆ And of course, coaching other people to pass on their new skills!

You should encourage the learner to make definitive plans for action to work towards these revised goals. You can help by moving into a **mentoring** relationship. A mentor has been described as:

One who guides without leading, teaches by example, and is willing to let the mentored one experience the bumps needed for learning and growth to take place.

Coaching Connection

Mentoring is a less involved relationship, one that is led more by the learner, who uses the mentor as a guide when they want guidance.

Who was the original Mentor?

Mentor is a figure in Homer's Odyssey. When Odysseus, the King of Ithaca went to fight in the Trojan War, he entrusted his son Telemachus to the goddess Athene, who disguised herself in human form as his trusted advisor Mentor. Homer tells us that her function was to become a friend, teacher and wise counsellor to Telemachus.

Evaluate the programme

You should also use this opportunity to review the coaching programme, to learn from it yourself. Both you and the learner should discuss the learner's experience of the programme and your own performance as a coach. You should have explained at the beginning what that role would be, but now is the time to review that. We said, in Chapter 1, that coaching is a process that guides someone towards an agreed set of goals, usually to improve their performance in a work role, and it mainly uses:

◆ Questioning

◆ Observing

◆ Listening.

In reviewing your performance as a coach you start by asking the learner to comment on how well you:

◆ Asked questions that led the learner towards improving performance.

◆ Observed his or her performance and provided useful feedback on strengths and weaknesses.

◆ Listened to what the learner had to say, especially to his or her questions, and gave useful answers and guidance.

You should also ask the learner:

◆ Which aspects of your performance as a coach had been particularly effective?

◆ Which aspects of your performance as a coach you should focus on improving?

As well as the learner completing the programme with an action plan, you should do as well. As a coach you should always be working on how you can develop and improve yourself as well as other people.

Ending the relationship

Your coaching may be mainly in short, one-off sessions that involve little relationship building. However, if you are serious about developing as a coach, you are will find yourself in longer term and more complex roles. If you have spent several weeks (or even months) coaching someone, you will have built up a bond that is hard to break. Such relationships can be:

◆ **Positive**, because they mean that you are communicating well and there is a likelihood the learner will be benefiting from it.

◆ **Negative** if the learner has become dependent on you and is unable to make basic decisions without consulting you.

The challenge is to ensure that you get the balance between an effective working relationship and one based on dependence. If at the end of the programme, you find that a learner has become too dependent on you, then you have missed the signs earlier on. You should look out for:

◆ Requests for advice on decisions the learner could make unaided

◆ A tendency for the learner to change opinions to match your own

◆ A tendency to contact you between coaching sessions

◆ A failure to perform effectively without your direct supervision.

Of course, not all these characteristics will appear, but if you see signs of any, and certainly signs of two or more, then you should be concerned. The coaching relationship can be described, in transactional analysis terms, as an adult : adult one. What happens in dependency situations is that the learner is trying to establish a parent : child relationship, and you need to refuse to play that kind of game.

Transactional analysis

Transactional analysis was popularised as a way of understanding relationships between two people by Dr Eric Berne, in his 1966 book *Games People Play*. Berne suggests that people can occupy one of three ego states when interacting with others:

◆ The **Child** state is one where people rely on instinctive responses, but also one that is dominated by our emotions and our need to be wanted and valued.

- The **Parent** state is one of nurturing others, but also of adopting learnt behaviours to cope with common situations, where we don't need to think too much.

- The **Adult** state is one that involves processing data and making decisions about complex issues, and to regulate the other two states.

When people feel under pressure or lack confidence in their ability to cope, they can adopt the Child state as a way of coping, passing the responsibility for decisions to others, seeking gratification through the approval of others. A coach who is faced with a Child state may easily adopt the Parent state in response. It means not having to think too much and simply giving directions. There is gratification in being looked up to by the other person.

Coaching is about dealing with complex issues of learning in a structured and developmental way. It is about two adults working together. To re-establish the Adult : Adult relationship, you should refuse to allow the other to be a Child and act as if he or she is playing the Adult role.

By the end of the relationship, if the learner has become too dependent, you have a responsibility to work together to resolve it. You may have a supervisor or mentor yourself who can help. Better still, watch out for the emerging pattern of dependence and take steps to prevent it becoming established.

Summary

In this chapter we have looked at record keeping, assessment, and two key issues for the end of a coaching programme. In particular we noted:

- The importance of keeping records and of involving learners in this

- The value of assessing learners' progress, and of doing so honestly, fairly and accurately

- That both formal and informal assessment involves judging a learner's performance against defined standards

- That assessment can be formative or summative

- Reviewing and evaluating the programme

- Ending the coaching relationship, ensuring that you have an effective (Adult : Adult) relationship with the learner.

7 The working coach

Now if we peel off these outer floppy leaves, we can sell what's left for twice as much – instant Iceberg!

The ethics of coaching

Ethics is concerned with morality (which is why it is sometimes called moral philosophy). In other words, it tries to distinguish what is right from what is wrong. Ethics is a very large and challenging area to explore, so we will focus on two key questions:

◆ What do you mean by 'right' (as in 'do the right thing')?

◆ How do you ensure that your behaviour as a coach is always 'right'?

Of course, this isn't only relevant to coaches – but coaches are different. They have influence over other people and often build up relationships that offers them the opportunity to do things that they may not get elsewhere. That's why coaches must be very clear about their personal standards of morality, so that:

◆ They know where to draw the line (to avoid taking advantage of their situation)

◆ They avoid inconsistency (so others will have confidence in them)

◆ They reduce their own doubts and increase their confidence.

What do you mean by 'right'

We all develop our personal sense of morality – of what is right or wrong – from many sources, but the earliest influences are most definitely:

◆ Our family

◆ The social environment in which we grow up

◆ The wider culture of which we are a part.

This process is called socialisation. We learn how to be part of society by learning its rules, and some of these are rules about what is right or wrong. These are sometimes referred to as our values or beliefs. Some- times we will base these on a religious faith, sometimes not, but they lie at the root of our behaviour and our attitudes – how we view the world.

However, there is one basic principle that seems to be common every- where, whatever the culture or religion, called the *ethic of reciprocity* or

'*The Golden Rule*'. This simply means 'treat others as you would like to be treated yourself'. You can use this as a handy rule of thumb in any situation where you aren't sure what is the right thing to do – how would you like to be treated if you were the person being coached. Don't simply do what you would want a coach to do for you, but use this knowledge to ask how the person you are coaching would like it to be done.

Knowing right from wrong

We all grow up learning what we should and shouldn't do, though sometimes we may do the right thing not because we feel it is right, but because we are afraid of getting caught and punished. In these cases our values may not be very strong. You should always be aware of what you believe is the right way to behave and try to live up to these standards, and not ask yourself 'Would I get away with it?'

Guidlelines for the coach

◆ Ensuring that the person you are coaching and the employing organisation are both clear about what you role is and the goals for the coaching activity.

◆ Being alert for conflicts of interest between the different people you are coaching and the organisations you work for (if you a freelance or work for a company supplying coaching services).

◆ Not using your position to take advantage of people. You need to be particularly alert to behaviour which may be seen to be discriminatory or offensive to people.

◆ Only doing what you know you are capable of doing. Don't be tempted to deal with issues that are outside your capability, whether this is to do with your technical competence in the topics you are coaching people about or personal issues or issues to do with relationships. Know your own boundaries, and also what other resources or services are available so you can refer people to these.

◆ Keeping proper records, and also be aware of the importance of confidentiality and security of information.

◆ Keeping yourself up to date and taking responsibility for your own personal and professional development.

Ethics and the coach

> **The European Mentoring and Coaching Council has a code of ethics that covers five main areas:**
>
> 1   Competence – this is about ensuring that the work you are doing is within your capabilities as a coach.
>
> 2   Context – this is about recognising that the people being coached and the sponsors (their employers, for example) each have their own expectations.
>
> 3   Boundary Management – this is about staying within your own capabilities and also being aware of potential conflicts of interest.
>
> 4   Integrity – this is about behaving honestly, safely and legally.
>
> 5   Professionalism – this is about not abusing the relationship with the people being coached in any way.

> **The Association for Coaching has a code of ethics and good practice that emphasises the importance of:**
>
> 1   Knowing your own abilities and limitations, and ensure that you continue to develop yourself and your knowledge of issues that will affect your work.
>
> 2   Establishing the basis on which the coaching contract is taking place, and the right to terminate it.
>
> 3   Being open about what the coaching will be like.
>
> 4   Behaving appropriately, being especially sensitive to issues of diversity and belief.
>
> 5   Keeping records of activity.
>
> 6   Monitoring the quality of the coaching, seeking feedback from learners and support from professional peers.
>
> 7   Being alert for any conflicts of interest.
>
> 8   Having professional liability insurance.

Have clear contracts

You may be an independent coach, or work for a coaching company, or coach people in your own organisation. It doesn't matter which, you still need to have clear contracts. These needn't be formal written ones – if you are coaching people in your team that would be absurd. However, you should make clear to the learner, and to anybody else who has an interest:

◆ What the outcomes are expected to be

◆ The likely timescales and when the coaching will occur

◆ Any record-keeping or reporting that is required

◆ Any payments to be made, when and on what basis

◆ Any health and safety, environmental or disability issues.

Be alert for conflicts of interest

Conflicts of interest can occur inside the organisation and between organisations.

Inside the organisation, conflicts of interest can arise because the learner, the line manager and the training manager may have different goals or expectations. The solution to these is usually openness – make sure everyone is clear that they differ in what they want the programme to achieve – and seek to find a resolution. This may mean trying to satisfy them all, or it may be about seeking a compromise.

Conflicts between organisations can occur if you are working for competitors. The opposite is true here – tell a client that you are working for a competitor but then explain that you must keep any further information completely confidential. Either the second organisation will prefer not to have you work with them or your emphasis on absolute confidentiality will convince them that you will keep their information confidential.

Be open about yourself but keep other people's confidences.

Behave appropriately

A coach will often work closely with learners, physically and emotionally. Both situations present opportunities for inappropriate behaviour, and a coach must be aware of this and make sure that they are above reproach.

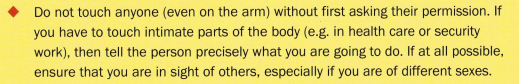

Guidelines for appropriate behaviour

◆ Do not touch anyone (even on the arm) without first asking their permission. If you have to touch intimate parts of the body (e.g. in health care or security work), then tell the person precisely what you are going to do. If at all possible, ensure that you are in sight of others, especially if you are of different sexes.

◆ Don't use inappropriate language. This includes the use of obscenities (however slight), derogatory, sexist, racist or similar terms, including comments that could be interpreted as such. It isn't about being politically correct or avoiding complaints or legal action (although that is something to be aware of), it's about being polite, professional and treating people with respect.

◆ Respect diversity. In some urban areas, there is an enormous ethnic, racial and religious mix of people. In other areas the population is far more uniform. Wherever you are, avoid making assumptions about people's backgrounds, beliefs and cultural norms – ask questions if you aren't sure about something (like how to pronounce someone's name) and remember the *Golden Rule*.

◆ Dress appropriately. Dress for the physical environment (an office, building site or factory) and for the culture of the organisation – its formality/informality. But err on the side of formality because the way that operatives dress may not be what is expected of coaches!

Work to your capability

Don't take on work you aren't capable of doing, and don't allow yourself to gradually move into areas outside your capability, especially if this involves counselling people on issues to do with their personal life. Coaches need to develop insight into their own abilities but also be aware of what they aren't able to do. They also need to develop their skills, but they should do this in a planned way so that they only start using their new skills once they are confident that they are able to do so competently.

Keep records

You need to keep records so that you can identify how well you are doing in meeting the agreed goals. You may also need to keep records for the organisation. You should be clear about what is expected and that the learner knows what is being recorded and who will have sight of it.

Records can contain a wide range of information, including:

◆ The outcomes of any preliminary diagnostic activities

◆ The goals agreed at the beginning of the programme

◆ Coaching plans

◆ Details of coaching sessions

◆ Progress reviews.

These records should be accurate, agreed with the learner, confidential and kept securely, cover only what is needed, and they should be used.

Develop yourself

A coach should be committed to personal development or else it would be very difficult to argue that others need to develop themselves. Have a personal development plan that identifies your:

◆ Personal and career goals over the short, medium and long term

◆ Actions that you will take to achieve them

◆ Reflections on what you have learnt.

Use Plan-Do-Review as the basis for your personal development and accept that it is your personal responsibility to make it happen.

Developing yourself

If you have got to this point then you must want to learn and develop yourself, or else why would you be reading the book? But there is a difference between learning and doing, and we will start by looking at what you have to do to convert what you know about coaching into being able to coach.

We saw very early on that there is a difference between *knowing that* and *knowing how*. This book is primarily about knowing that, but has also tried to help you turn what you know into practice, to know how. However, you need to work on that aspect yourself.

In Chapter 2 you were introduced to David Kolb's theory of the *learning cycle*. His argument is that you need to work your way round the full cycle for true learning to occur. This book has has encouraged you to:

◆ Observe and reflect on experience

◆ Form abstract concepts.

You now have to:

◆ Test out those concepts

◆ Have concrete experiences.

How you do that depends on your work role, the kind of coaching you want to do and who you will be doing it with. Below we'll look at how you can plan to do that, but first we'll look at a further source of help in turning *knowing that* into *knowing how*.

Using feedback

Feedback is a valuable way to learn. It is particularly valuable when you are trying to turn what you know about a role into reality. Your role as a coach involves providing feedback to learners to help them learn and improve; it also works in reverse. Their feedback can help you to improve your performance as a coach. This feedback can be formal or informal:

◆ **Formal feedback** occurs when you invite learners to describe to you their experience of your coaching.

◆ **Informal feedback** from learners is always available to us but we don't always receive it, either because we aren't alert to the signals, or don't want to acknowledge it if it shows us under-performing. As a coach, you need to be particularly alert to the signals others send. This is one of the characteristics that marks out effective coaches - they are responsive to their learners and able to develop themselves as they develop others.

Action planning

By reflecting on your experiences and on the feedback that you have received, both formal and informal, you can refine and improve your performance, turn what you know about coaching into effective practice. This means identifying those aspects of the role or techniques that you need to try out or to improve, and planning what you need to do to achieve this – a sequence we have already described as *Plan-Do-Review*.

The only person who can make this happen is you! You need to plan what you are going to do to develop and improve, to practise what you have learnt – to turn *knowing that* into *knowing how*. So here are some key questions for you to think about – and answer – now, to help you move from learning about coaching to doing it:

Activity

◆ What do you think you would be able to coach people to do?

◆ Where would you be able to undertake this coaching?

◆ What do you need to do to make this happen?

◆ Whose help do you need to enable you to do this?

This is your plan for putting what you have learnt into action. It's not very complicated, but it is important that you know the answers to these questions. You also need to decide when you are going to take these actions, and set yourself some firm goals for making it happen – in other words, some **SMART goals**.

The only problem with taking responsibility for your own learning is that it is very lonely. Without sufficient motivation you can easily give up. That's why it's useful to have people to help.

Who can help you?

If you are a manager or team leader and want to coach team members or other employees, then you will probably need the support of line managers and possibly people in the training and development team. If you have to make a case for getting involved in training, then it may help if your employer subscribes to any of these standards:

◆ **ISO 9000** (the international standard for quality management)

◆ **Investors in People** or IiP – the UK's standard for organisations that are committed to training and developing their people

◆ **European Framework for Quality Management** or EFQM – the European standard for organisations committed to excellence, which includes people development as a core element.

These and others place great emphasis on the importance of learning and development to maintaining the required standards. But your organisation doesn't have to use external standards to believe in the importance of coaching. Managers should welcome your commitment to coaching if they are committed to:

◆ Quality and continuous improvement

◆ Health and safety at work

◆ Motivating employees to work to their full potential

◆ Retaining high performing employees.

Of course, you may not be intending to use coaching in your own workplace.

◆ You may work as a trainer or assessor, and want to develop your coaching skills to add to the range of work you can do. In particular, if you work with apprentices or trainees on S/NVQ programmes, then coaching is a valuable skill to have, to help them develop their workplace competence.

◆ You may not yet be in a training or development role, but want to move into one. In that case, you should look for opportunities to develop your practical skills so that you are able to demonstrate that you have the ability to take on such a new role.

113

Whatever your role, you need to be clear about how you can help the organisation achieve its goals through coaching and then you'll be far more likely to get the help and support you need.

Being supervised

A key principle for all coaches is the concept of supervision. A supervisor is someone who takes responsibility for your development as a coach. Peter Bluckert, who runs a successful coaching business, says that coaching supervision should offer a coach three benefits:

◆ The opportunity to **reflect** on what you have been doing as a coach, to make sense of what has happened and help you work better in future.

◆ To gain **support**, in the form of ideas and suggestions on how to deal with situations or people, and to get emotional support if that's needed, because coaching can become quite stressful when you deal with people with real problems.

◆ To help your **continuing learning and development**, by hearing about other people's ideas and experiences.

Who should be your supervisor?

There are various people who could take the role of supervisor.

◆ If you join a training course in coaching, then the course providers may well offer supervision as part of the programme. Your **trainer or tutor** may well provide a supervision service for some time after the formal training sessions are completed.

◆ If you work for an organisation that actively supports coaching (either as part of its internal development strategy or as an independent coaching provider) then you may well find that they have a **formal supervision scheme**. This could be through senior coaches in the organisation, or through peer supervision.

◆ **Peer supervision** means that a group of coaches work collectively to support each other. Although they may lack some experience, so limiting the opportunity to draw on their depth of knowledge, they will probably understand your experiences and feelings better.

◆ Peer supervision may operate as an **Action Learning Set**, which is a structured way of peer support for learning. The big advantage of Action Learning is that you collectively take responsibility for each person's learning.

Action Learning Sets

Action Learning was developed in the 1950s by Professor Reg Revans and he emphasised that it was a very simple idea – that we learn best by working together in a group to help each other to find solutions to real work problems by discussion. The way Revans expressed his model was through an equation:

Learning = Programmed (or expert-provided) knowledge + Questioning

In other words, we learn best when our learning is driven by enquiry (questioning) supported by access to the knowledge and experience of those who have come before us – accessed through learning resources and expert tutors. Instead of learning being driven by trainers and tutors, it is driven by the need to resolve real problems. This really motivates people to learn.

◆ A **personal support network** could also provide you with a source of supervision. You may be able to find a friend or work colleague who is willing to spend some time with you occasionally, to talk through your experiences. Although limited, such a person is likely to be best at giving you the emotional support you may need in first getting into coaching, when you will feel anxious and uncertain.

◆ Last but not least, don't forget your **family**. A spouse or partner, brother, sister or parent can provide you with the emotional support you need when starting out on a new task or job role. Their support is often vital and something we take for granted yet often aren't aware of until we need it most.

Your future career

Is coaching going to be another string to your bow, or the basis of a completely new career? Many people start coaching because it seems a useful technique, often without even thinking of it as being something different from their normal work role. All too often people who fall into coaching like this, treat it as being one-to-one training (a *telling style*). One of the major lessons you should have taken from *Coaching* is that this is only appropriate with low-skilled unmotivated learners. If you treat coaching as a significant vehicle for developing people and improving performance, and want to make a worthwhile change in people's lives and in the organisations you work for then you will be interested in what role coaches can have.

◆ The **manager as coach** – this has become an increasingly important approach in organisations employing highly skilled people in fast changing workplaces. Managers have become less concerned with command and control, more with coaching and continuous improvement. If you are (or want to be) a manager or team leader, then coaching is a vital skill for you to develop, alongside development as a leader and manager.

◆ The **trainer as coach** – we've already seen how people working in workplace training, whether inside organisations or as external trainers, are using coaching as a way of developing competence and improving performance. Again, you can develop your coaching skills as a way into this role, or to extend your role if you already work as a trainer. As well as coaching you will also need to be trained as a trainer, especially on publicly funded programmes (as a condition of funding).

◆ The **life, business or executive coach** – if you see yourself becoming a full-time coach, working with individuals and companies to help people address job performance, career development and personal development issues, then you will find that skills or technical coaching is a good way to start. The skills of coaching are transferable skills; once you have developed them then you can use them in a range of contexts. However, before you get into life coaching or into business or executive coaching, you need experience of life, business and management! You may also find that it helps to be trained and qualified in areas like psychology or counselling, or in management and leadership, to help you perform in the role effectively.

Two important things to remember:

1   Coaching is first and foremost a practical skill, and like all practical skills it requires practice. However, it also needs a thorough understanding of the coaching process and of the tasks and subject matter in which you are coaching people. Start slowly and work to develop yourself. Success comes to those who are motivated and willing to learn.

2   Anyone can call themselves a coach. There are qualifications available, and associations and networks you can join to help you establish yourself and also to introduce some quality standards into a fast-growing industry. Look carefully at these, talk to other people who are coaches and find out how they can benefit you and the people you coach.

Summary

In this chapter we have looked at the ethical issues facing a coach. You must:

◆ Ensure that the learner and the organisation are clear about your role and the goals.

◆ Be alert for conflicts of interest.

◆ Not use your position to take advantage of people.

◆ Only do what you know you are capable of doing.

◆ Keep proper records.

◆ Take responsibility for your own personal and professional development.

Self-development is particularly important. You need to:

◆ Turn what you have learnt about coaching (knowing that) into practice (knowing how).

◆ Seek support from your managers, a supervisor or your peers or friends.

◆ Have some vision of where you want to go, as a coach.

Whatever your vision of yourself in years to come, your future as a coach starts here. Good luck!

Index

I.S. L&D London Life T-210

Coaching
April 28, 2008